COCOA: AN EXPLORATION OF CHOCOLATE, WITH RECIPES

SUE QUINN

Photography by Yuki Sugiura

Hardie Grant

QUADRILLE

CONTENTS

"The mingled scents of chocolate, vanilla, heated copper and cinnamon are intoxicating, powerfully suggestive; the raw and earthy tang of the Americas, the hot and resinous perfume of the rainforest. This is how I travel now, as the Aztecs did in their sacred rituals. Mexico, Venezuela and Colombia. The court of Montezuma. Cortez and Columbus. The food of the gods, bubbling and frothing in ceremonial goblets. The bitter elixir of life." —Joanne Harris, *Chocolat*

Chocolate. No other food has the same beguiling, delicious pull on our senses. Almost magically, and alone among the things we eat, chocolate melts at around body temperature, flooding our mouth with voluptuous sweetness, an array of flavours and a whisper of bitterness as soon as we place it on our tongue. Its chemistry lights up the pleasure centres in our brain, energizes us and sates our hunger. But chocolate is more than just an edible delight.

Chocolate is nostalgia. A simple bite into a favourite bar can carry us back to our first childhood treat, that sweet reward for good behaviour or the comforting snack when we were sad. Chocolate is also full of contradictions. It's a balm for heartache yet also a symbol of love and desire. It's redolent of luxury, but more often than not produced by some of the poorest people in the world. It was revered by the ancients as a sacred gift from the gods, but legend also holds that chocolate was a powerful aphrodisiac that fuelled Casanova's orgies and empowered Montezuma to satisfy his harem. Over the years, chocolate has at once been hailed as wholesome, nourishing and medicinal, and also a vehicle for women to poison men and practise witchcraft.

Each bite of chocolate is imbued with history and flavoured with its epic journey over millennia from the rainforests of the Amazon, where the ancients first discovered how to prepare bitter cacao seeds, to the freshly minted bars stacked on supermarket shelves today.

Chocolate is infused with politics and imperialism, economics and slavery, transport and technology, society and culture. It has fed the imaginations of artists from Salvador Dalí to William Hogarth, and inspired writers from Samuel Pepys to Enid Blyton.

Globally, we now consume more than $US100 billion worth of chocolate confectionery every year, according to Euromonitor. But how did the bitter cacao bean become one of the world's most adored foods?

The chocolate that we devour so eagerly today is a product of our age. Modern technology, integrated transport networks, global trade and—bitter sweetly—war, slavery and colonial expansion, were needed to make it possible. Because, in the beginning, there was no chocolate, just the curious bulbous pods that dangled like vivid lanterns from the trunks of *Theobroma cacao* trees.

These distinctive plants originated in the lush cloud forests of the Upper Amazon. Archaeologists are learning more about humans' long love affair with chocolate every day, but the most recent evidence suggests the Mayo Chinchipe-Marañón people of modern-day Peru consumed cacao as far back as 3500 BC, probably as a drink made with maize and chilli. How they first came to unlock the magic of the bitter purple beans, we will probably never know exactly. Perhaps they copied the monkeys and squirrels they saw in the treetops, who ripped open the pods and devoured the pulp inside. But rather than toss away the seeds, as some animals did, the ancients discovered that by grinding them on a stone—a tool they used to prepare many foodstuffs—they could transform the beans into a remarkably rich, sticky and aromatic paste: the first chocolate.

Humans eventually transported cacao north from the Amazon to Mesoamerica (which encompassed parts of modern day Central America and Mexico), where the Olmec people and then the Mayans developed a rich chocolate culture. Much of the mythology that surrounds the chocolate we eat today can be traced to the Mayans. These culturally advanced people, whose civilization flourished between AD 250 and 900, developed a hieroglyphic writing system to record their lives in gorgeously illustrated folding books (codices) and on ceramic vases, pots and drinking vessels. An abundance of these ceramics still exists, as well as four codices, all referencing and depicting cacao being harvested, prepared and consumed. Traces of theobromine, a chemical component of cacao that can survive for centuries, have also been found inside some vessels and on ceramics.

These artefacts confirm that cacao was much more than just a foodstuff to the Mayans and later the Aztecs: it was sacred and magical. Mayans believed cacao came from the Underworld and they placed it at the centre of their economic, political and ceremonial lives. The elite sipped cacao drinks—both 'green' ones made from fresh pulp and others made from roasted and ground beans—to seal marriage vows and to mark important life events like marriage and the birth of children. They also buried the drinks with the dead as sacred offerings to gods and patrons. Recent evidence suggests some of the ancients might have consumed cacao in food, as well.

The Mayans and Aztecs also used cacao beans as a form of currency. They dried and fermented the beans, which preserved them, and being small and light, they were ideal objects to transport and exchange. It was, in fact, on a Mayan trading canoe that Christopher Columbus first encountered cacao beans during his fourth and final voyage to the New World in 1502. But when he captured the vessel on Guanaja, an island of Honduras, he assumed the beans were almonds. Writing about the encounter in his diary later, Columbus's son Ferdinand observed that the Mayans placed a high value on what appeared to be prosaic objects: "They seemed to hold these almonds at great price; for when they were brought on board ship together with their goods, I observed that when any of these almonds fell, they all stopped to pick it up, as if an eye had fallen." But Columbus thought nothing of the 'almonds' and sailed away in search of gold. He had no way of knowing he had just become the first European to encounter cacao and had turned his back on one of the great gastronomical discoveries of all time.

It took another seventeen years, with the arrival of Spanish conquistador Hernán Cortés and his forces in the New World in 1519, for Europeans to begin to understand the true importance of cacao. The Spanish noticed that the Aztecs used the beans as specific units of currency (one turkey was worth 100 beans, an avocado 3, and so on), and stored vast quantities in royal warehouses and strongholds (which the conquistadors duly plundered). The Mayans and Aztecs both used annatto, the seeds of the achiote tree, to colour their cacao drinks red to resemble blood, which had a central place in Mesoamerican cultures. Spanish observers also famously claimed that Aztec Emperor Montezuma II drank copious amounts of chocolate from golden goblets in bacchanalian fashion to seduce women. But historians say there is no evidence he drank chocolate for its supposed aphrodisiac qualities; it's possible the drinks had simply fermented to the point of being alcoholic.

Originally, the Spanish found cacao's bitterness repulsive, "more a drink for pigs than a drink for humanity," according to one observer. But cacao eventually found its way to Spain in the late sixteenth century, where the royal court added sugar, cinnamon and other familiar ingredients to suit their palates. Meanwhile, Spanish colonists in the New World also acquired a taste for the drink, and chocolate culture crossed the New World/Old World divide.

For a time, the Spanish considered chocolate such a prized luxury that they kept the secret to themselves. But word quickly spread. Jews, driven from Spain and Portugal by the Inquisition, took the skill of grinding chocolate with them, many to France, where they developed the chocolatier culture. Meanwhile, Jesuit and Dominican missionaries travelled between the New World and the major cities of Europe, spreading word of chocolate far and wide, as well as the ingredients and paraphernalia to make it. The chocolate secret was out.

Within one hundred years of the Spanish conquest, chocolate was being quaffed in the royal courts and grand homes of Baroque Europe, and by the seventeenth century also began to make its way into cookery books. Soon, chocolate was being included in an array of dishes from sorbets, mousses and cakes through to savoury plates. Meanwhile, a pot of hot chocolate became a feature of the breakfast table in England and France — at least for those whose fortunes afforded them the luxury of a sumptuous morning meal.

By the end of the seventeenth century, the chocolate craze had spread across the upper and middle social classes of Europe, and beyond. Until recently, historians believed the Spanish, and then the English colonists, took cacao beans to North America. But new evidence suggests that chocolate was consumed as a drink in North America 1,000 years ago, having found its way there via a trading route stretching from New Mexico to Central America.

But while the global appetite for chocolate grew, cacao production in Mesoamerica slumped, as indigenous populations were decimated by European diseases. Production soon shifted to South America, where plantations were serviced by multitudes of slaves shipped in from European colonies in West Africa. Europeans also spread cacao to their colonies in the tropics — with the Dutch, British and Germans clashing with the Spanish for possession of cacao-rich territories.

Chocolate remained almost exclusively a drink until the mid-nineteenth century, when the Industrial Revolution delivered machines that transformed it from a luxury beverage into an affordable mass-produced snack that almost everyone could enjoy. While European chocolatiers masterminded chocolate's evolution from gritty drink to meltingly delicious bars and confections, US entrepreneurs perfected its mass production. Milton Hershey was among the first in the world to invest heavily in chocolate-making machinery in the late nineteenth century and went on to build his own factory town in Pennsylvania and Disney-like theme park based on chocolate. His empire continues to thrive, and Hershey's Kisses are one of the most popular chocolates of all time.

Cacao never really made an impact in the Middle East, possibly because coffee was so popular that chocolate as a drink couldn't gain any ground. Neither did it catch on in India, Southeast Asia and the Far East in those early days. (One exception was the Philippines, a Spanish colony between 1543 and 1898, where it is still grown and used in Philippine cuisine).

By the early twentieth century, chocolate had taken the form of the bars and filled confections that we're familiar with today. From those first few beans that made their way from Mesoamerica to Spain more than 500 years ago, cacao has ballooned into a global commodity that is grown in the shade of equatorial forests right across the 'cocoa belt', from Fiji all the way to Mexico. Annual production of cacao now totals around 4.5 million tonnes a year.

As our taste for chocolate has grown, the starring role of cacao has faded. Milk, sugar, and vegetable fats (first added to chocolate during the Second World to stop it melting easily in the desert heat, and widely used ever since), now overshadow the rich complex flavours in the beans. Sometimes, these additives mask defective and inferior cacao in mass-produced chocolate, according to experts. Today, the global chocolate market is dominated by multinational companies — including Mars, Ferrero, Mondelēz, Nestlé and Hershey — whose priorities are to produce identical tasting bars as cheaply as possible.

Fortunately, over the past twenty years or so, a small but important chocolate revolution has begun. Hundreds of 'bean-to-bar' and craft makers around the world have started producing small batches of chocolate from scratch, often using cacao beans from a single country or region. Using a similar approach to producing wine, coffee and olive oil, this new generation of chocolate makers employs methods designed to showcase the essential flavours of the cacao beans. The makers speak of 'terroir', 'single origin', 'flavour profiles' and notions of 'purity'. Some prioritize fair trade and the ethical sourcing of beans and labour.

It's a welcome movement in many ways. But the division of chocolate into cheap mass-produced bars versus more expensive fine versions — in other words, 'good' or 'bad' — might not be universally welcome. Everyone's love of chocolate is deeply personal, anchored in memories, food experiences, taste preferences and budget. Who is to judge which chocolate deserves praise or opprobrium? What is certain is that when the revolution started in the early 2000s, chocolate had shifted a very long way from its ancient roots, to the point where the original, essential, magical, complex and delicious ingredient — cacao — had almost been forgotten. A chocolate renaissance was long overdue.

CACAO OR COCOA?

The name *Theobroma cacao* was devised in 1753 by Carl Linnaeus, who created the naming system that we use for all living things. *Theobroma* is the Greek word for 'food of the gods' — no one is sure which gods he had in mind, but one theory is that he simply loved chocolate.

The Spanish probably derived the word *cacao* from the Olmec/ Mayan term *kakawa*. Most sources agree that the word *chocolate* is derived from the Nahuatl (Aztec language) word *chocólatl*, which referred to 'cacao water' or beverages made with cacao.

The difference between the words *cocoa* and *cacao* is more problematic. In the UK, the term *cocoa* refers to the unadulterated powder made from ground beans that is called *cacao powder* in the US. It's thought the difference came about by error; one theory states that the printers of Samuel Johnson's *Dictionary of the English Language* accidently ran together the entries for *coco* (coconut) and *cacao* — and the error endured.

Even more confusingly, convention has it that *cacao* refers to the plant, beans and fruit before processing, while *cocoa* refers to the processed, powdered product. For the sake of simplicity, this is the way the two words are used in this book.

"The Scharffen Berger bars tasted like chocolate, too, but they also tasted like bright raspberries and roasted nuts, creamy caramel and coffee — all just from the cocoa itself." — Todd Masonis, *Making Chocolate: From Bean to Bar to S'more*

For a very long time, chocolate sold in supermarkets and convenience stores remained steadfastly, resolutely the same. Large-scale chocolate manufacturers launched new products now and then; milk, white or dark (and a few different shades thereof) was the extent of the choice when it came to bars. Splashing out on 'good' chocolate meant buying bonbons or truffles from pricey chocolatiers in luxe packaging on special occasions, and then the stars of the show were often the fillings. The flavour of the actual chocolate, the provenance of the cacao that went into it, and the beans' journey to the bar were of little consequence to most consumers. For a long time, I never gave these issues a second thought.

But around 20 years ago, a new chocolate movement came to life, stirred by two French companies. In 1983, Bonnat, founded in 1884 and still a family-run business in the southern French town of Voiron, had launched a range of 'origin' bars, each made with cacao beans from a single country. Valrhona, founded in 1922 and based near Lyon, had partnered with Robert Linxe, the iconic founder of the La Maison du Chocolat chain and launched Guanaja, the first origin bar in its 'Grand Cru' range, in 1986. Initially made as 'couverture' for chefs and chocolatiers, chocolate lovers quickly discovered these Grand Crus were very delicious to eat, too. For many years, Valrhona was the chocolate maker of choice for top pastry chefs, home bakers and chocolate aficionados, and is still hugely popular today. But the chocolate scene was about to change.

In 1997, Americans John Scharffenberger, a wine maker, and Robert Steinberg, a doctor who loved European chocolate, built a chocolate factory in Berkeley, California under the name

Scharffen Berger—and quietly started a revolution. They opened their doors to the public, most of whom had never seen chocolate being made before. For Todd Masonis, co-founder and CEO of Dandelion Chocolate, now a leading 'bean-to-bar' maker based in San Francisco, the experience was a revelation. "In a big way, Scharffen Berger reclaimed flavour. It jogged our cultural memory with a simple reminder that chocolate was more than a single, classic, brownie-like note. Chocolate could—and should—have complexity, nuance, tone and *flavour*," he writes in the Dandelion book, *Making Chocolate: From Bean to Bar to S'more*.

In 2005, to the dismay of some of the craft chocolate makers it had inspired, Scharffen Berger was sold to US confectionery giant Hershey, but the seeds of the fine chocolate movement had been sown. Enthusiasts started to make bars in small batches in their kitchens and garages, using repurposed and/or vintage equipment. Some of these craft makers expanded into commercial operations, making chocolate on a micro-batch and medium-sized scale, innovating as they grew. Brothers Rick and Michael Mast, who founded the Mast Brothers chocolate company in Brooklyn, New York, in 2007, are widely credited with popularizing craft chocolate in the US.

The fine chocolate sector is still tiny; only 5 per cent of the world's cacao production is considered 'fine' according to the International Cocoa Organization (ICCO) definition. But recent estimates suggest the number of fine, craft or artisan chocolate makers has boomed over the past decade to around 1,000 in the US, and more than 30 in the UK.

WHAT EXACTLY IS FINE CHOCOLATE?

There is no official definition but, in broad terms, fine chocolate makers transform high-quality cacao beans into chocolate in-house, with the primary aim of coaxing out the best possible flavour. Much like wine, the flavour of chocolate reflects the climate, soil and other environmental factors—the *terroir*—of the region where the cacao beans were grown, as well as their genetic profile. It also carries the fingerprints of the people who ferment and dry the beans, and the chocolate makers who bring them to life through roasting and processing. Every batch of cacao has its own personality, and fine makers strive to draw out the finest features of its character.

It is a completely different approach to large-scale producers, who use bulk or commodity beans, mainly from the Côte d'Ivoire and Ghana, which are interchangeable in terms of flavour. This enables them to achieve consistency in their mass-produced bars and to sell them cheaply. The price that industrial-scale chocolate producers pay for beans is extremely low; the commodity price for cacao was around $US2.20 per kilogram at the time of writing, according to the ICCO. And farmers receive much less than this—as little as 75 per cent on average, according to some estimates. What's more, mass-produced chocolate is often made with inferior beans and has preservatives, flavourings and vegetable fats added to cover up defects, keep costs low and maximize shelf life.

The ICCO produces a list of countries where beans with 'fine' attributes grow. At the time of writing, the most popular origins were Madagascar, Dominican Republic, Peru, Ecuador, Bolivia and Belize, and fine beans from these countries are celebrated for their flavours, which might include fruit, floral, herbal, wood, caramel or nut notes. However, not all the beans from these origins are 'fine' quality, and excellent beans come from other places, too. So, another body, the not-for-profit Heirloom Cacao Preservation initiative, is attempting to identify cacaos that make the most flavourful chocolate based on their genetic profile and to conserve these varieties for the future. But it is important to remember that even the best beans can be ruined in the wrong hands.

Fine chocolate makers often buy cacao through small brokers or directly from farms or cooperatives, and generally pay a premium. This, combined with their smaller scale can make fine chocolate—like fine wine—more expensive than mass-produced bars. The most expensive fine chocolate can cost £20 [$US25] per bar or more, but most range between £4 and £7 [$US5–9].

The smallest-scale fine chocolate makers produce in batches of just a few kilograms, which enables them to experiment with beans, blends and production techniques. This can result in more interesting, complex chocolate.

Fine chocolate must contain over 60 per cent cocoa solids for dark, over 30 per cent cocoa solids for milk and, for unflavoured bars, no added ingredients other than extra cocoa butter and sugar. A few purists, like Dandelion, add only sugar to what is known as 'two-ingredient chocolate'. Other makers pepper their bars with 'inclusions' that reflect and/or complement the natural flavour profile of cacao beans. In California, Dick Taylor adds garlic, seeds and salt; in the Hudson Valley, Fruition ages beans in bourbon staves; in New York City, Raaka steams beans over simmering Cabernet Sauvignon. Meanwhile, in the UK, Duffy Sheardown, a former Formula One engineer, deploys the same scientific approach to chocolate as he did to shaving fractions of seconds off lap times, producing some of the world's finest single origin bars in the process. In Wales, Pablo Spaull of Forever Cacao crafts fine vegan chocolate from unroasted Peruvian cacao using coconut milk. And in Suffolk, Pump Street has applied the same meticulous approach to making fine chocolate as it did to mastering the art of naturally leavened bread (page 18). These are exciting times for chocolate lovers.

Until recently, chocolate was rarely made in regions where cacao grows, and some people involved in its production have —still—never tasted it. Regrettably, this geographical divide between well-off consumers and poor producers has been a feature of chocolate's story from the beginning. But the fine chocolate movement has seen the emergence of 'tree to bar' chocolate makers in the equatorial belt where cacao grows. Makers like Pacari in Ecuador, Menakao in Madagascar, Shattell in Peru, the Grenada Chocolate Company and others are now producing some of the world's finest chocolate. This movement might finally enable cacao growers to share in the vast profits generated by the world's insatiable appetite for chocolate.

Chris Brennan is a self-confessed science geek and inventor. Fed up with being unable to find decent bread 'anywhere in England' and with time on his hands after retiring from his job at IBM, he set out to make the perfect sourdough loaf himself. After tinkering with flours and starters in a makeshift bakery in his garage, he began selling loaves from a local market. In 2010 he opened Pump Street Bakery in Orford, a tiny idyllic village in Suffolk. It is now one of the UK's most acclaimed artisan bakeries and cafés. Then he applied the same rigorous approach to chocolate.

His first attempt in 2013 was a disaster. "Being Jamaican, my vision at the time was to make great Jamaican chocolate," he recalls. "I paid £600 for a sack of beans but the first bars tasted like fungus, so I threw the whole lot out and started again." The scientist in him kept experimenting (he studied chemistry at university) and he soon realized that meticulous sourcing of beans was key. Not only did they have to be the finest quality but the farmers needed to care about the fermentation process and understand its impact on the final flavour of the bar. Now, he only imports beans directly from the best farmers in places like Ecuador, Grenada, Jamaica, Honduras and Madagascar — and pays three to four times more than farmers generally receive outside the direct trade system.

Brennan also developed a unique way of roasting beans that drew on his baking experience. The beans are put through two roasts: one using steam at a very high 240°C [464°F], and a second roast at a lower temperature. "I think a good percentage of what we've created comes from the way we roast," he says. "No one does it the way we do." The chocolate is also left to mature for 30 days before tempering to allow the flavours to develop and any lingering acidity to evaporate.

Many awards later, Brennan, 74, strictly controls the production process with his daughter Joanna. In 2017, their small factory turned out 25 tonnes [26 tons] of chocolate — still relatively 'tiny', but production is increasing at a rate of 60 per cent a year. Early on, Brennan realized that the yeasts and bacteria used to make sourdough bread were the same ones involved in the fermentation of cacao beans. To prove his point, on a recent trip to the Caribbean Island of St Vincent, he collected some of the liquid run-off from the cacao fermentation process. He brought it back to the UK, fed it with flour and turned it into natural leaven, which is now used to make bread at the bakery. He also came up with the idea of squaring the bread-chocolate circle in a bar.

"We thought, if they have the same genesis, why don't we put bread back into chocolate? Everyone puts chocolate into bread, why don't we go the other way?" The result is their hugely popular Sourdough and Sea Salt bar that combines two signature products: dark chocolate and sourdough crumbs.

"The cocoa woods were another thing. They were like the woods of fairy tales, dark and shadowed and cool. The cocoa pods, hanging by thick short stems, were like wax fruit in brilliant green and yellow and red and crimson and purple." — V. S. Naipaul, *The Middle Passage: Impressions of Five Colonial Societies*

In 2018, I visited the jungles of Tabasco, Mexico, to get up close and personal with chocolate trees. It could have been all the cocoa I had consumed that had gone to my head, but I sensed a little bit of magic in the sweet steamy air. The wrinkled elongated seed pods of *Theobroma cacao* dangled from the tree trunks like alien eggs, in pale yellows and greens through to vibrant oranges and burgundies, according to variety and maturity. Intercropped coconut, banana and mango trees dappled the pods in shifting shadows. Underfoot, a thick carpet of leaf litter nourished the trees and harboured fungi that protected them from disease. The forest floor was also a breeding ground for midges, the tiny insect pollinators without which chocolate trees could not exist.

There, in the Jesús María plantation near Comalcalco, the cacao trees were thriving, and it was easy to assume that *Theobroma cacao* is robust and hardy. The truth is, chocolate trees are fussy creatures. They only grow in the equatorial belt around 20 degrees north and south of the equator — and normally less than 700m above sea level. They demand shade, humidity and deep, rich, well-drained soil. They dislike temperatures cooler than 16°C [61°F] and are prone to disease.

VARIETIES

Most reference books still classify *Theobroma cacao* into three groups: *criollo*, *trinitario* and *forastero*, but this approach is now considered outdated. In recent years, as scientists have been able to peer into the cacao genome, it has emerged that things are much more complicated. The term *forastero* simply means 'foreigner' in Spanish, but DNA analysis has made more precise identification possible. In 2008, Juan Carlos Motamayor, a cacao scientist with the chocolate giant Mars, led a team that identified ten distinct genetic 'clusters' or 'varieties' of *Theobroma cacao*. Since then, the number has steadily grown. In reality, however, *Theobroma cacao* is promiscuous, and the beans are often a tangled web of genetics.

That said certain varieties of cacao often appear on fine chocolate bars.

CRIOLLO
is often defined as the 'best' and is highly prized for its flavour and lack of bitterness. *Criollo* is low-yielding, disease prone and the beans are rare, so the chocolate it goes into can be the most expensive.

NACIONAL
also known as Arriba, is found in Ecuador and northern Peru and is known for its floral and fruity flavour.

ARMELONADO
is a prolific strain that forms the basis of most West African 'bulk' cacao.

TRINITARIOS
are named hybrids, of which there are many hundreds. The name comes from Trinidad, where the first blending of varieties happened.

Lots of generalizations are made about the flavour of chocolate made with beans from specific 'origins'. For example, Madagascan chocolate is famed for being fruity, while bars from the Dominican Republic typically have a 'chocolate pudding' character, according to connoisseurs. In reality, a single region can produce beans with different characteristics.

The fruit of the cacao (or chocolate) plant Theobroma Cacao

CACAO VARIETY CCN-51

Cacao variety CCN-51 is contentious. Cloned to be high-yielding, fast producing and resistant to disease, some cacao farmers, notably in Ecuador, turned to CCN-51 to save their livelihoods after weather and disease threatened their crops. Some chocolate analysts believe countries risk becoming too reliant on this one crop, as small producers abandon higher quality, more flavourful, heritage varieties. But others believe that with careful processing, and in the hands of skilled chocolate makers, it can yield high-quality bars.

"In my mouth the chocolate broke at first like gravel into many separate disagreeable bits. I began to wonder if I could swallow them. Then they grew soft, and melted voluptuously into a warm stream down my throat." — M.F.K. Fisher, *The Art of Eating*

Chocolate is a miracle. Nature's bounty and human ingenuity have intertwined over millennia to turn what appear to be unpromising ingredients — hard bitter beans — into the world's most craved food.

The journey from tree to bar begins when the trees are 2–4 years old, and thousands of tiny, delicate blossoms start sprouting directly from the branches and trunk of each tree. Only a tiny percentage of these blooms survive to be pollinated and grow into pods, which take 5–6 months to mature. Farmers must keep track of individual pods to determine when they are ripe, and they harvest them twice a year. They do this by carefully cutting the lower pods off with a machete, making sure not to damage the buds from which more will sprout; they use a *palanca*, a knife attached to a pole, to reach the higher ones. There is no place for modern machinery in the harvesting of cacao.

The farmers cut open the pods to reveal 30–50 beans nestled in a sticky white pulp. (If you ever get the chance to eat this pulp, seize it: it's a fresh, tangy and delicious cross between lychee and lime. In some cacao-producing countries, drinks made from the pulp are a hugely popular antidote to the tropical heat.) As soon as the beans are exposed to the air, they start to ferment.

FERMENTATION

Fermentation generally happens on the farm where the cacao is grown. Farmers place the beans and pulp in boxes, hanging bags or pile them onto banana leaves, then cover and leave them for

2–8 days. Natural yeasts kickstart the process, then lactic acid bacteria take over. Farmers turn the fermenting beans over to aerate them every 1–2 days, sometimes more, when the lactic acid bacteria are succeeded by acetic acid bacteria. Mikkel Friis Holm, an award-winning Danish chocolate maker known for experimentation, has shown how small changes to the fermentation process can have a big impact on chocolate flavour. He famously created two versions of his Chuno bar made with Nicaraguan beans: one where they were turned twice during fermentation, and another with beans turned three times. The two bars taste distinctly different.

DRYING

After fermentation, farmers traditionally spread the beans out in the sun to dry on mats, trays or terraces. In industrial processing, forced air dryers are sometimes used; in wet regions like Papua New Guinea, drying is sometimes done over open fires, imbuing the chocolate with a distinct smoky flavour. Once the beans have been dried, they are cleaned, bagged and shipped to chocolate makers.

From this point, the process depends on whether the beans are destined for large-scale manufacturers, where nuanced flavour is not important, or fine chocolate makers. Fine chocolate makers tend to experiment, sometimes using a combination of old, new, domestic and commercial equipment and their own secret tricks to produce distinctive bars.

ROASTING

Chocolate makers select, sort and in some cases, blend the fermented and dried beans, then roast them to develop the flavours. Unroasted beans are still dominated by acetic acid, so the Maillard reactions that occur in the oven (browning, which delivers flavour) round out and develop the beans' complexity. Roasting too quickly or unevenly can destroy some of the beans' intrinsic flavours and produce chocolate that tastes burnt. (This can, however, be a question of taste: some British connoisseurs believe French makers generally over-roast their beans, masking some of the more complex and delicious flavours.) Whole beans are usually roasted for 30–60 minutes at 120–160°C [248–320°F], sometimes more.

Advertisement for Bensdorp's cocoa, showing a Dutch woman pouring herself a cup

The roasted beans are then cracked and winnowed; the papery shells are blown away, leaving behind broken up beans, called nibs. Often, chocolate makers put the nibs through a grinder to turn them into a peanut butter-like paste. They then transfer this paste to refining machines fitted with stone or heavy metal rollers, along with other ingredients, according to the style of chocolate they are making: sugar for dark chocolate (bittersweet or semisweet in the US); sugar and milk solids or powder for milk chocolate; flavourings such as vanilla, cocoa butter for extra creaminess and soy lecithin (an emulsifier that helps make smooth chocolate).

Over the course of hours or days, depending on the maker, the cacao particles are rolled and ground very fine. The heat generated in the process melts the cocoa butter fat, transforming the mixture into a voluptuously thick and shiny liquid known as cocoa mass or liquor. Some makers then strain this to remove any undissolved sugar. Pump Street Chocolate (page 18) is an example of a maker who then stores the chocolate at a controlled temperature for a month or so, to allow the flavours to develop.

In industrial processing, conching is a separate step where the chocolate is stirred and aerated to develop flavour. Smaller makers, however, often use the same machine to refine and conch. These are commonly CocoaTown machines, based on traditional Indian spice grinders. Industrial-scale chocolate makers also employ different techniques to deliver flavour and extend the shelf life of their bars. Cadbury, for example, combines sugar with condensed milk and some cocoa mass, which is then dried together to produce a 'crumb', which has a very long shelf life. The crumb is processed with more cocoa mass, cocoa butter, emulsifiers and flavouring, and then conched. Large manufacturers often remove some of the cocoa butter and sell it to the cosmetics industry, then replace this with vegetable fats including palm oil.

TEMPERING AND POURING

To ensure a shiny finish and a good snap, chocolate must be tempered to control its transition from liquid to solid—see page 42.

"Try to recall the smell of foods you like (such as freshly baked bread or pungent cheeses) or the aroma of nature itself: flowery, herbal, spicy. Remember the smell of a gush of rain on a hot street pavement, the tempting scent of ripening fruit, or the disturbing pungency of slightly rotten fruit." —Maricel E. Presilla, *The New Taste of Chocolate*

"Hold your nose," instructs Cat Black. On her cue we spoon some melted chocolate into our mouths and taste without smelling, quietly considering what's happening in our mouths. Contrary to the deliciousness my brain is anticipating, it's an anticlimax: I can detect a slick of chocolate across my tongue and some vague sweetness, but almost no flavour.

After a few moments, Cat signals to let go of our noses. Whoosh! As the aroma molecules waft from my mouth to the back of my nose, they fire the nerve signals that tell my brain about the different compounds in the chocolate. Suddenly there's a flood of flavours: rich chocolate, a little bitterness, some bursts of fruitiness. And just when I think the flavours are fading, I detect a wave of something else. Is it coffee? "You can see that a lot of the subtlety of the flavour of chocolate is in the aroma," Cat says. By some estimates, only 10–20 per cent of what we perceive as flavour comes from our taste buds—the rest is delivered through our nose.

Cat has the kind of covetable job careers advisers never tell you about at school. A chocolate expert and judge in international chocolate competitions, Cat also lectures at the International Institute of Chocolate and Cacao Tasting (IICCT) in London—and she is teaching us how to taste chocolate like professionals. As I will learn on this Level 1 course, tasting chocolate like a connoisseur is challenging and not just a matter of devouring different bars to see if we can notice the difference. Chocolate lovers like Cat would like more of us to learn to appreciate the complex flavours of fine chocolate—the 'notes of origin', as some aficionados describe it —because there is so much more to enjoy than in mass-produced bars. Fine chocolate—made from high-quality cacao beans that are often from a single origin (country or region)—is a world away from cheap chocolate confectionery (although that has its place, too).

Fine chocolate's flavour is like a completed jigsaw puzzle, where pieces have been added at each stage of cacao's journey from the tree to the bar. When we place a piece of chocolate in our mouth, we are tasting the genetic profile of the beans; the soil, climate and environment where they grew; the care (or otherwise) with which they were nurtured and harvested; the fermenting, roasting and other processes that turned them into chocolate. The beans themselves deliver astringent and bitter notes, and then the fermented pulp delivers fruity, winey and flowery flavours. Roasting and Maillard reactions give rise to a symphony of toasted, nutty, floral and spicy notes. Conching balances out these flavours, and then milk, sugar and other ingredients might be added. The flavours in chocolate comprise hundreds of aromatic compounds.

Appreciating all the nuances takes practice and focus—and a good palate. At one stage on my course, classmates agreed there was a note of 'unripe banana' in the chocolate we had just tasted. Everyone, that is except me: I had no idea what they were talking about. But Cat stresses there is no right or wrong way to eat chocolate, and the aim should be to enjoy it. Flavour is notoriously subjective; we all appreciate food differently, through the prism of our personal preferences, food culture, memories and physiology.

But connoisseurs have devised a structured approach to chocolate tasting that uses all the senses to detect the subtleties of flavour and texture. Obviously, you don't need or even want to eat chocolate this way all the time, but it's a fascinating and delicious thing to try.

You don't have to buy expensive chocolate. These days, many supermarkets sell a range of high-quality 'single origin' bars. Specialist chocolate suppliers and makers also offer ranges that enable you to enjoy an interesting variety of flavours and textures.

Avoid tasting chocolate straight after eating strongly flavoured food—that spicy curry might prevent you from detecting some of the subtle notes—and clear your palate by drinking water before you start. On the IICCT course we were given soft polenta.

First, look at the chocolate and notice whether it's light or dark. Although there are no 'best' colours, the shade might indicate the percentage of cacao, the kind of beans used, how they were roasted (a very dark or black colour might indicate over-roasting, for example) and whether ingredients like milk have been added.

The surface of well-made chocolate should, generally, be smooth and shiny, indicating the cocoa butter has been properly crystallized (tempered). A 'bloom' on the surface — white or light-coloured splotches — can occur if the chocolate has come into contact with moisture or has not been tempered correctly. It might also tell you the chocolate has melted and solidified again, for example, after being left out in the sun. (Bloomed chocolate might not be pleasant to eat but is perfectly safe.) Also notice how the chocolate breaks: a clean snap is another sign of proper tempering.

SMELL THE CHOCOLATE

Now, smell the chocolate. Aroma is an important but often neglected part of appreciating flavour, as Cat's exercise demonstrated. That is because our tongues can only recognize the five basic tastes: sweet, salty, bitter, sour and umami (often described as savoury). Flavour is delivered through aroma compounds that have two routes to the brain: via our nasal passages when we sniff food (orthonasal olfaction) or via our mouths when we eat and breathe out (retronasal olfaction). Both ways, receptors in the nose receive the aroma molecules and send signals to the brain that allow the identifications of flavours. Interestingly, the brain detects flavours differently depending on whether we're breathing in or breathing out, so we need to do both when tasting chocolate.

To smell chocolate most effectively, hold it up to your nose and sniff and breathe several times; some people recommend holding it in cupped hands, like you might sniff brandy from a balloon glass. Cat suggests making a note of your first impressions. "Your most immediate gut reaction is very important, if only just to tell you whether you like it or not," she explains.

TASTE THE CHOCOLATE

Now, place a small piece of chocolate in your mouth. "Let it melt, don't munch," says Cat, echoing the IICCT's mantra urging chocolate tasters to take their time. Allowing the chocolate to melt in your mouth, perhaps chewing it a little to break it up, enables aroma molecules 'trapped' by the cocoa butter to escape and drift into your nasal cavity and through to the olfactory receptors. Quickly devouring chocolate wastes some of the interesting flavours.

OBSERVE THE TEXTURE

Notice the texture of the melted chocolate in your mouth; generally, the smoother it feels, the more it has been refined, but this is not necessarily a sign of quality. Some high-quality small-scale makers produce chocolate that is not as smooth and silky as mass-produced versions, simply because they are making it in small batches with different machinery. (Some chocolate, Mexican-style versions, for example, is intended to be slightly coarse.) There might be a fatty sensation in your mouth, due to the addition of too much cocoa butter; an unappealing waxy sensation might suggest that fats other than cocoa butter have been used, like vegetable oil.

CONCENTRATE ON THE FLAVOURS

Focus on the flavours as they develop and change. Breathe out through your nose with your mouth closed and different aromas will come to you in stages; some people refer to this as a flavour 'journey'. Are there tiny bursts of fresh fruit and if so, do they remind you of anything specific, like banana, raspberries, stone fruit or lemons? Are there spicy notes like black pepper, cloves or liquorice? Maybe you can detect a nuttiness that reminds you of almonds or hazelnuts? Or there could be roasted flavours such as tobacco, burnt caramel or coffee.

Chocolate can also have defects that make it taste bad or flavourless. Some varieties of cacao simply taste bland or very 'earthy'. But beans can also be affected by mould, which imparts a musty flavour, or contaminated with chemicals or smoke. If beans

have been over-fermented they might have a 'cheesy' flavour, and if under-fermented, taste flat or like 'cardboard'. Over-roasting can make chocolate taste bitter and burnt.

Cat says another thing to look for when tasting chocolate is the balance of the tannins. These are naturally occurring compounds in cacao beans (also in grape skins) that create a dry, bitter, astringent sensation in the mouth. These come from compounds that are part of cacao's natural defence against being eaten by predators, and it is normal to detect them in chocolate. The finest chocolate makers balance the tannins with good flavour (and get the fermentation, roasting and other processes right) so they do not leave an unpleasant, mouth-puckering dryness.

After you swallow the chocolate, think about the aftertaste—
some of the best bars deliver a series of flavours, some which linger
for 20 minutes or more. Remember that whatever you taste or
experience, no one's appreciation of chocolate is wrong. Food likes
and dislikes are shaped by social and cultural factors, your food
history and even what your mother ate while she was pregnant.
We taste with our hearts and minds as well as our tongues. In fact,
a number of chocolate aficionados I spoke to while researching
this book recommended ignoring the flavour notes printed on
chocolate wrappers. "I hate being didactic about the flavours
people 'should' find," Cat says. "Different people, different food
cultures, have different reference points for taste. I want people
to be open to the notion that there may be a journey when they taste
chocolate and be attuned to it." Really, the most important thing
is: do you like it?

DIFFERENT FLAVOURS

Our senses detect hundreds of chemicals when we taste chocolate.
Once we decide whether we like it or not—the amygdala part of
our brain tells us whether it is safe to eat—we sort the flavours
into 'archetypes' or groups based on our own personal experiences.
But flavours are incredibly hard to describe: being able to detect a
flavour is much easier than putting a name to it. So, here are some
descriptors that might help you.

Fruity: Red berries, tropical fruit, dried fruit, stone fruit, citrus
Earthy: Wood, hay, soil, olives, nuts, herbs
Caramel: Butterscotch, brown sugar, molasses, toffee
Floral: Jasmine, orange blossom, rose
Dairy: Milk, cream, yogurt, butter
Toasted: Espresso, smoke, tobacco, burnt
Spicy: Black pepper, cloves, nutmeg, cinnamon, liquorice, vanilla
Cocoa: Brownie, cocoa powder, dark chocolate, fudge, chocolate milk
Nutty: Hazelnuts, almonds, walnuts, peanuts, sesame

Award-winning master chocolatier Paul A. Young is a maverick when it comes to flavour: he's famous for experimental pairings, like Marmite truffles or bonbons infused with tobacco. And he's also a free spirit when it comes to tasting. He might make some of the world's finest handmade chocolates and regularly judge at international awards, but he often takes a relaxed approach when tasting a new chocolate for the first time. "If we were having a taste now, I wouldn't give you any instructions and tell you not to chew and let it melt in your mouth," Young says, as we chat in his chocolate shop in London's Soho.

He says deciding whether you like a chocolate and identifying what appeals to you about it, is similar to a new relationship: you need a few dates to get to know each other. "When I get a new chocolate from a producer I live with it for two or three weeks, and just eat a bit a few times a day just to get to know it," he says. "My palate's different morning, noon and night."

He finds it's better not to over-think the process, so he performs mundane tasks while he eats some. "Although I've learned to be technical with chocolate, I still find I get the most out of it by eating it creatively," he says. "For me, this means I eat some, put it down, go and do other things like the ironing, and an idea will eventually come to me."

He believes there's no room for snobbery when it comes to chocolate: whether you enjoy mass-produced bars, bite the top off a bonbon first and scoop out the caramel with your tongue or pop the whole thing in your mouth at once, it's up to you.

"Your palate is yours and everyone does it differently," Young says. "Do you like the taste? Is the aftertaste nice? Would you want it again even if you are stuffed full? For me, that's what chocolate tasting is all about: do I want another piece?"

"You would rather have six bars of bad chocolate than one bar of good chocolate. Why? Why are six bad things better than one good thing? I don't understand." — Jenny Colgan, *The Loveliest Chocolate Shop in Paris*

There are endless ways to enjoy chocolate, but the choice can be baffling. Here's how to differentiate the fine from the faux.

FINE CHOCOLATE

There's no technical definition for fine chocolate; it is produced on large and small scales. But you can tell a lot (although not everything) from information on the wrapper. It should state the country of origin of the beans (ideally the name of the cacao farm), who the chocolate maker is and sometimes tell the story behind the bar (but beware of marketing hype).

For unflavoured bars, the list of ingredients should include nothing other than cocoa or cacao beans, cocoa butter, sugar and vanilla (not vanillin or vanilla flavour). Soy lecithin is widely added too; it makes it easier for chocolate makers to work with and has little effect on flavour. Remember, ingredients are listed in descending order by weight, so if sugar is first and you are looking for fine chocolate put down the bar—this is not it.

Chocolate makers sometimes use the term 'bean to bar'. This is accepted to mean that they ship in the picked, fermented and dried beans, ideally buying directly from a farmer, and then make the chocolate from scratch on their own premises, from roasting to wrapping the bars. This is distinct from makers who buy in cocoa mass (also known as cocoa liquor), a smooth paste made from ground roasted beans. If 'cocoa mass' appears on the ingredients list, the maker is not genuinely 'bean to bar'.

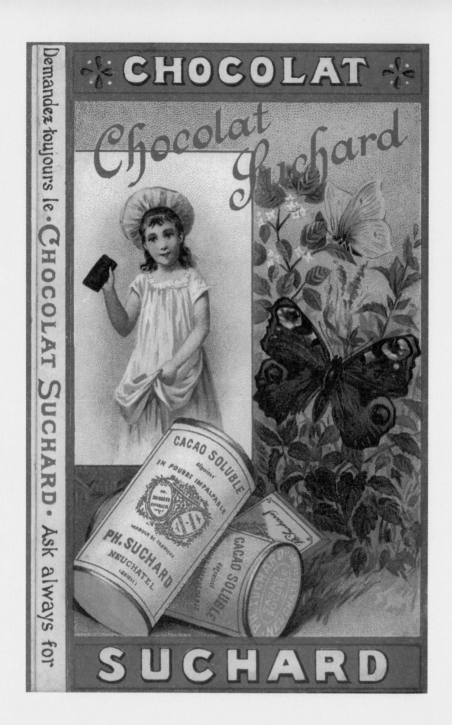

Chocolat Suchard, Neuchâtel, established in 1826

'Tree-to-bar' chocolate is made in the region where the beans are actually grown and harvested. There are very few producers in the world who do this, but they are worth seeking out to support the growers, workers and local economy.

Ideally, find out as much as possible about the producers before you buy. Also, try to ensure the supplier is trustworthy and beware of chocolate made in bulk and packaged to give the impression of being fine, 'bean to bar' or artisan. There are increasing numbers of imposters out there.

INDUSTRIAL PREMIUM CHOCOLATE

Industrial premium chocolate, including some top-of-the-range supermarket-brand bars, are marketed as fine, but often do not live up to the hype. Check the ingredients list before you buy to ensure you are getting what you are paying for and what you want. That said, decent mass-produced premium bars are fine to use in cooking but probably will not have the beautiful flavour characteristics of fine chocolate.

CHOCOLATE CONFECTIONERY

The vast majority of the world's cacao—up to 95 per cent by some estimates—goes into mass-produced confectionery and candy bars (as well as ice cream, cakes, desserts and snacks). These are the bars that many of us grew up with and love, but the reality is they contain very little cacao, as low as 20 to 25 per cent, in the case of milk chocolate. What is included is bulk cacao from West Africa. Some experts say defects in the cacao are hidden by large quantities of sugar, vegetable fats and other additives.

PERCENTAGE COCOA SOLIDS

The cocoa percentage on chocolate wrappers causes much confusion, but in theory at least, it is straightforward. The figure tells you how much of the bar by weight is made from cacao beans, including any extra cocoa butter the maker added (which is very common). For example, an unflavoured bar that states 75 per cent cocoa is made from 75 per cent ground up cacao beans with the possible addition of extra cocoa butter, and 25 per cent sugar.

Generally, the higher the cocoa percentage, the less sweet and the more intense the chocolate tastes. But the figure does not tell you the proportion of cocoa butter in the bar. This is one reason why two chocolate bars with the same cocoa percentage can taste completely different: one might be less intense and sweeter because it contains more cocoa butter. The key thing is, the percentage has no bearing on quality.

MILK CHOCOLATE

In the US, milk chocolate must contain a minimum 10 per cent cocoa, and in the UK and Europe 20–25 per cent. Some manufacturers lightly caramelize the milk solids or dried condensed milk to add flavour. Sugar is always added, and generally soy lecithin too, to improve the flow properties of the chocolate. Dark milk chocolate is now growing in popularity. These are bars with a much higher percentage of cocoa than traditional milk chocolate.

DARK, PLAIN, SEMISWEET AND BITTERSWEET

Dark or plain chocolate are UK terms for semisweet or bittersweet chocolate in the US, which contains no milk solids. Traditionally, bittersweet has less sugar than semisweet, but the levels of sweetness and bitterness are determined by the manufacturer, so they are interchangeable in baking. Dark/plain/semisweet/bittersweet chocolate must contain a minimum 35 per cent cocoa, but often has more; a wide range of percentages are available, and these are stated on the wrapper. Sugar is added, and often extra cocoa butter, lecithin and vanilla or vanillin (artificial vanilla).

UNSWEETENED OR 100 PER CENT

Used in baking, and more widely available in the US than in the UK and Europe (although this is changing), unsweetened or 100 per cent chocolate contains no sugar, and often has a coarser texture than lower percentages. It is ideal for savoury cooking when you want to use chocolate simply as a spice or to add richness.

COUVERTURE

Couverture (meaning 'covering' in French) is dark chocolate with a relatively high cocoa butter content (at least 32 per cent), which makes it more free flowing when melted, and easier for chefs and chocolatiers to use for dipping, pouring and moulding. Once tempered and hardened, it also gives a glossy sheen and a good snap. If you don't have couverture to hand, most premium brands of dark chocolate, chopped, work perfectly well. They are, in fact, probably couverture without being labelled as such.

Aside from the expense, there is no reason why you cannot use fine chocolate in cooking (except, perhaps 'two-ingredient chocolate', as it has no extra cocoa butter added and can be difficult to melt and work with). Complex chocolate works beautifully in simple desserts where the flavours can shine through, like a soufflé or mousse, for example. Chocolate with particularly notable flavours works well with complementary ingredients. Madagascan chocolate with vibrant berry notes works beautifully in a chocolate and raspberry tart, for example.

CHIPS

Some chocolate chips (or morsels) are designed to hold their shape when baked into cookies and cakes. They contain a lower percentage of cocoa butter and, sometimes, other forms of fat. Baking-resistant chocolate chips, by definition, do not melt well, so avoid substituting them when other forms of chocolate are specified in a recipe.

IMPORTANT!

When a recipe calls for chocolate with a specific percentage of cocoa, avoid deviating too far from this. Delicate flavours that work beautifully with 60 per cent cocoa will be overwhelmed by a chocolate of 85 per cent or more. Substituting chocolate with lower/higher cocoa percentages changes the amount of sugar in the recipe and can radically alter the texture of a cake or cookies, for example.

Nibs are crushed and cracked roasted cacao beans that have had their skins removed, and are an increasingly popular chocolaty ingredient in their own right. Intense and aromatic, good-quality versions deliver delicious bursts of cocoa flavour, as well as a softly crunchy texture. I often add some to porridge and to infuse milk, cream, hot beverages and alcoholic drinks with a pleasant cocoa flavour. They taste delicious sprinkled over salads or in cakes and biscuits (either whole or ground). Nibs are widely available in supermarkets, online and in speciality shops but just like chocolate bars, quality can vary.

COCOA POWDER

Cocoa powder is made from ground cacao beans from which most of the cocoa butter has been extracted. The powder does contain some fat, anywhere between 8–26 per cent, depending on the brand.

In Europe and the UK, cocoa powder is usually 'dutched', a process named after the Dutch chocolate pioneer Coenraad van Houten. An alkaline substance, potassium carbonate, is added to the cacao beans, which neutralizes their acidity and gives them a milder flavour and darker colour. The treatment also enables the cocoa powder to mix with liquids more easily. Some purists prefer 'natural' cocoa powder, the most common kind available in the US. They argue that the alkaline treatment imparts an unpleasant taste and destroys some of the roasted, caramel notes.

Generally, dutched and natural cocoa are not interchangeable in baking. Because the acidity of Dutch-processed cocoa has been neutralized, it does not react with alkaline raising agents, such as bicarbonate of soda, so no carbon dioxide is generated, and bakes might not rise. All the recipes in the book were tested using Dutched cocoa powder.

WHITE CHOCOLATE

Some enthusiasts get into a lather about white chocolate, arguing that it is not technically chocolate. I take a more relaxed view: as it contains cocoa butter, a component of cacao beans, it counts, as far as I am concerned. (Legally, white chocolate must contain at least 20 per cent cocoa butter.) White chocolate also contains milk solids, sugar, vanilla and sometimes soy lecithin.

BELGIAN CHOCOLATE: THE MYTH

Chocolate makers sometimes emblazon their wrappers with 'Belgian chocolate', as if it were a mark of quality. It is not. A whole range of factors contributes to chocolate's quality and flavour, but the country where the chocolate is manufactured is no yardstick. Belgium does have a tradition of making lovely filled chocolates and bonbons, but the actual chocolate is not necessarily any better than that made in other parts of the world.

RAW CHOCOLATE

The popularity of 'raw chocolate' is rising, due in part to its supposed health benefits. Because the beans are not roasted, manufacturers claim they retain more healthful antioxidants than conventional chocolate. Sceptics argue that during fermentation, the beans can reach temperatures well above the limit set for raw food. And some observe that it is necessary to blast the beans with heat to kill dangerous bacteria, such as salmonella and E. coli. My advice? Chocolate is not a health food, even if it is made from 'raw' beans, so choose your chocolate for its quality and flavour.

STORING CHOCOLATE

Chocolate bars should be kept in a dry environment, ideally at 14–20°C [57–68°F], so that means not in the fridge (too moist and cold). Avoid fluctuations in temperature, so the cocoa butter fat does not melt and recrystallize. Chocolate usually has a long shelf life and will keep for 18 months or so. It readily absorbs other smells, so rewrap open bars in foil and keep inside a sealed bag.

"Chocolate is one of our most remarkable foods." — Harold McGee, *On Food and Cooking: The Science and Lore of the Kitchen*

As an ingredient, chocolate's personality is unique: it possesses certain quirks that are both loveable and challenging at the same time. For example, chocolate not only delivers flavour and richness to a dish, it can also provide the structure. (Cocoa particles contain starch and fat, so by adding eggs for moisture and setting purposes, it is possible to make a chocolate cake without any flour.) But accidentally splash a tiny amount of water into the chocolate as you melt it and the glossy pool will seize and transform to a gritty mass. Understanding the science will help you work with it in the kitchen.

MELTING CHOCOLATE

Chocolate is a poor heat conductor, so for easy melting, chop it into very small pieces first or blitz to a crumb in a food processor. This way, as much of the surface area as possible is exposed to heat.

There are several ways to melt chocolate, but whichever method you find most convenient, be sure not to let it get too hot. Heating chocolate to higher than around 45°C [113°F] can destroy the emulsifying agents, commonly lecithin, which manufacturers add to make it flow and melt easily. Overheated chocolate can 'curdle' — the cocoa butter will start to separate from the cocoa solids — and turn grainy. Dark chocolate, being just cocoa solids, cocoa butter and sugar, can be melted and solidified repeatedly. Because milk chocolate contains milk solids, it should be melted more gently.

Some people find it convenient to melt chocolate in a microwave, although I think it can be difficult to control the temperature. If it is your preferred method, heat the chocolate in

Advertisement for Fry's pure breakfast cocoa, showing a little boy carrying a tin of cocoa through the snow with his dog

short bursts on a low/medium setting, stopping to stir it frequently. Take the chocolate out when most but not all of it is melted. Stir until it's smooth and completely melted. How long this takes will depend on your microwave and the chocolate you are melting.

Melting chocolate on the stove gives you more control over the heat. Place the chopped chocolate in a heatproof bowl set over a pan of barely simmering water. Alternatively, to be sure the chocolate does not overheat or come into contact with steam, pull the pan of simmering water off the heat and then place the bowl of chocolate on top. Stir until melted—this keeps the temperature even. Do not let the bottom of the bowl touch the water; the chocolate at the bottom of the bowl will get too hot and seize. When you remove the bowl from the pan, make sure none of the steam curls into it, as the moisture can cause problems, too.

MOISTURE AND CHOCOLATE

A tiny amount of moisture can spell death to a batch of melted chocolate. Yet adding hot liquid to chocolate—traditionally cream, but also water, fruit juice and alcohol—is how you make ganache. According to food scientist, Harold McGee, it works like this. If you add a small amount of water or steam to melted chocolate, the water molecules form droplets that act as a kind of glue, wetting the sugar and cocoa particles enough to stick them together into patches of syrup, which separate out of the liquid cocoa butter. However, adding enough liquid to dissolve all the sugar, rather than just wet it, allows the chocolate to retain its smoothness and flow.

TEMPERING

Melt a bar of chocolate and then leave it to harden, and it will look and feel different before and after. The reset chocolate won't be as shiny as it was before it melted; it will be a little soft and crumbly, and possibly dull and streaky. This happens because the chocolate's shine and snap are determined by the alignment of the cocoa butter crystals. Cocoa butter exists in six different crystalline forms and only one arrangement really delivers the perfect chocolate finish. To achieve this ideal alignment, the chocolate must be tempered, or melted and reset in a controlled way.

Award-winning British chocolatier Kerry Witt shared with me a technique that's ideal for home cooks who want to obtain quite small amounts of tempered melted chocolate—as little as 100g [3½oz] or so—without actually doing any tempering. It works because most commercially available chocolate has already been tempered: by warming it gently and carefully it melts but retains some of the desirable cocoa butter crystals. All you need is a hairdryer.

Chop your dark or milk chocolate (not too finely or it will blow away) and place it in a heatproof bowl (ideally plastic, not metal) and set your hairdryer to high. Direct the hot air at the chocolate for 30 seconds. Stop the hairdryer and stir the chocolate well, then repeat the heating and stirring until the chocolate melts. To check if it is ready to work with, dab a little on your lip: if it feels slightly cooler than body temperature (if you have a thermometer around 31–32°C [88–90°F] for dark chocolate or 30–31°C [86–88°F] for milk chocolate) it should be ready. If it feels too warm, set it aside for a few minutes, and repeat the lip test until the chocolate is cool enough. Alternatively, spread a thin layer on a piece of foil or acetate or the back of a spoon. Tempered chocolate should set in a few minutes, and have a smooth and silky surface. (The side in contact with the surface will be shiny.)

You will have to use the chocolate quickly—if it begins to set before you have finished, fire up the hairdryer and warm it again.

TROUBLESHOOTING
· When melting chocolate, don't add anything cold or it may seize.
· Add hot liquid all at once to solid chocolate rather than adding it gradually to melted chocolate.
· If a recipe requires adding a small amount of liquid, add it to solid chocolate and melt the ingredients together. This includes butter, which contains a significant percentage of water.
· If adding liquid to melted chocolate, a good rule of thumb is to make sure it is warm and measures at least 1 tablespoon per 55g [2oz] melted chocolate.
· If chocolate seizes because of moisture, add more hot liquid or boiling water a teaspoon at time and stir fiercely until smooth.
· To save overheated chocolate that has seized, try stirring in a little solid chocolate, cocoa butter or even vegetable oil, and/or use a stick blender to smooth out the chocolate.

"Waked in the morning with my head in a sad taking through the last night's drink, which I am very sorry for; so rose and went out with Mr. Creed to drink our morning draft, which he did give me in chocolate to settle my stomach." — *The Diary of Samuel Pepys*, 24 April 1661

Of all the health claims made about all the foods, the wondrous powers of healing attributed to dark chocolate are among the most tantalizing. Throughout its history, chocolate has been claimed to have curative benefits; in fact, many of the earliest chocolatiers started out as apothecaries, enrobing medicines in chocolate to make them more palatable. But in modern times, dark chocolate seems to have shifted dramatically from treat to miracle cure, at least if the headlines are to be believed. As I researched this book and explored the bottomless ocean of articles propounding its health benefits, it was clear why many people believe dark chocolate is good for them. All we need to do, the articles state, is sit back and enjoy a delicious square or two to stave off cancer, lower blood pressure, reduce the risk of heart attack, and enhance our cognitive powers — to name just a few conditions it can supposedly ward off or cure.

But are any of these claims based on robust scientific evidence? Given that most people love the taste of chocolate, are we simply indulging in wishful thinking? Are the big chocolate manufacturers encouraging us to feel this way by pouring millions of pounds into research that invariably finds positive links between the compounds in cocoa and human health? Or were the ancients, who possessed vast knowledge of the healing power of plants, on to something when they administered cacao as a medicine?

Historical records show that from earliest times, cacao has been used for healing. The Aztecs consumed it both as beans and ground into a paste for drinks (sometimes with other medicinal herbs added) to treat an array of complaints, from digestive problems to skin disorders. They even scattered the flowers of the cacao tree in perfumed baths to give them energy.

After conquering the New World in the sixteenth century, the health-obsessed Spanish acknowledged that Aztec medical practices were more advanced than their own, rooted as they were in a detailed knowledge of plants. Once cacao arrived in Spain, physicians slotted it into the prevailing 'humoral theory' which, in its simplest terms, categorized diseases and the plants that cured them into the four humours: hot, cold, moist or dry. Confusingly, chocolate fell into more than one category, depending on how it was administered. But it was generally agreed that chocolate was beneficial to health when taken in modest amounts.

Over the course of the following centuries chocolate was consistently hailed by scientists, physicians and thinkers as a cure and therapy for dozens of conditions, as well as a drink that could be appreciated for its taste. Numerous treatises written during this period claimed chocolate could fatten and nourish the weak, energize the exhausted, and improve digestion, bowel function and a range of other ailments. In the eighteenth and nineteenth centuries, chocolate was widely held to promote longevity, and French gastronome Jean Anthelme Brillat-Savarin declared it could improve brain power.

THE POWER OF ADVERTISING

But just as today's chocolate companies try to tempt us into buying their products by projecting a wholesome image (the iconic picture of the glass and a half of milk is still prominent on the front of every Dairy Milk bar), cocoa purveyors of the past were inclined to a little propaganda.

Chocolate was an expensive, strange and not entirely delicious drink when it first arrived in London in the seventeenth century. Historian, Dr Matthew Green, who conducts tours of London's erstwhile chocolate houses, has written that chocolate needed a good marketing campaign to propel sales in those early days. "A slew of pamphlets appeared proclaiming the miraculous, panacean qualities of the new drink, which would boost fertility, cure consumption, alleviate indigestion and reverse ageing: a mere lick, it was said, would 'make old women young and fresh, create new motions of the flesh'," Dr Green wrote in the *Telegraph* newspaper. "The commonest claim, however—one inherited from the Aztecs and still perpetuated by chocolate companies the world over today—was that chocolate was a supremely powerful aphrodisiac. The public was sold on this mendacious publicity campaign."

Today, chocolate companies, like all food manufacturers, are prevented by law from making wild health claims like these. But with sales of milk chocolate stalling in recent years, as consumers become more health conscious, big chocolate manufacturers have poured vast sums of money into chocolate science, to explore the links between cocoa and human health. These studies have often been reported in the media with wildly exaggerated claims. And chocolate companies have done little to correct public perceptions that dark chocolate is a health food.

1920s advertisement declaring the generous milk content in every half-pound Cadbury's Dairy Milk Chocolate bar

There's certainly promising evidence that chemical compounds found in cacao beans called flavanols may have properties beneficial to human health. Two in particular, epicatechin and catechin, have captured scientists' interest. Professor Ian Macdonald, an expert in cocoa flavanols from Nottingham University, says these were once thought to be antioxidants—molecules that inhibit cell damage through oxidation. But scientists now believe flavanols serve a different function. Professor Macdonald says cocoa flavanols increase the production of nitric oxide in blood vessels, which improves blood flow. "In theory, this should reduce blood pressure and some studies have shown this, in long-term treatment of people with mildly elevated blood pressure," he says. And a growing body of research suggests these chemicals might lower the risk of cardiovascular disease. One recent study found that people who ate chocolate three times a month had a reduced risk of heart failure compared to those who ate none. But researchers said eating too much also carried health risks and more studies were needed. Likewise, there is some evidence that brain function in people with cognitive impairment might be improved after taking cocoa flavanols, although other studies have failed to back this up.

Professor Jeremy Spencer, a world leader in flavanols and brain function at Reading University, tells me there is good evidence that cocoa flavanols might temporarily boost our powers of concentration due to increased blood flow to the brain. (This might also explain why chocolate can improve our mood). "You find improvements in cognitive performance on specific tests that involve attention, sustained attention and sustained focus on complex tasks," Professor Spencer says. "It happens in healthy individuals across all age ranges, and we see the effects during the one or two hours after consuming the cocoa flavanols." The newest and most exciting area of research is exploring how flavanols, including those found in cocoa, are broken down in the gut. "There's a lot of interest in how this impacts the population of bacteria in the gut and how this, in turn, effects the immune system," he says.

All this falls a long way short of the health claims made in the media about dark chocolate being a virtual cure-all. As yet, there is no robust scientific proof that consuming cocoa flavanols reduces our risk of heart attack, improves our health or extends our lives: long-term studies would be needed for that.

One such study is underway. In 2015, Mars began its five-year Cocoa Supplement and Multivitamin Outcomes Study (COSMOS) in conjunction with Harvard Medical School. Involving 18,000 men and women in the US, it is investigating whether daily supplements of cocoa flavanols or a common multivitamin can reduce the risk of heart disease, stroke and cancer.

Crucially, study participants are not eating chocolate. Like most recent 'chocolate' studies, COSMOS is using a form of cocoa flavanols that are much more concentrated than those found in commercial chocolate bars and powders. That is because cocoa flavanols are partly or completely destroyed in the chocolate-making process. As a general rule, dark chocolate contains more flavanols than milk chocolate. But contrary to popular belief, the quantity of flavanols does not increase with the darkness of the chocolate. Rather, the flavanol content depends on the variety of cacao beans used and the way they were processed. Milk chocolate contains virtually no flavanols.

Even Mars concedes that chocolate is "not a good delivery mechanism" for flavanols. "They are largely destroyed during the manufacturing of chocolate," a spokeswoman for Mars told me. "Chocolate therefore contains negligible amounts of flavanols, no matter the amount of percentage of cocoa." The aim of the COSMOS study is to explore the benefits of cocoa flavanol supplements.

The truth is, we would need to eat vast and unhealthy amounts of dark chocolate to consume enough flavanols to have any beneficial effect, according to scientists. A 2016 German study found that a daily 100mg dose of epicatechin—the amount that reliably causes an improvement in blood flow—was the equivalent of up to 200g [7oz] of chocolate. And the 900mg of flavanols that achieved lower blood pressure in some people was the equivalent of up to 500g [1lb 2oz] chocolate. Scientists, and even Mars, agree that chocolate is too calorific and sugar-laden to be a healthy delivery vehicle for these 'nutrients'.

Of course, savouring a square of dark chocolate is much healthier than devouring a bar of milk chocolate loaded with sugar, added fats and chemicals. You will want to eat less of it anyway, because it is richer and more intensely flavoured. Studies have also shown that dark chocolate can attenuate hunger more than milk and white chocolate, and the pleasure gleaned from delicious food is good for our overall wellbeing. But there is no proof—so far—that dark chocolate will prolong your life. Sad but true.

TO WARM
AND SOOTHE

WHIPPED MEXICAN-STYLE HOT CHOCOLATE
WITH CINNAMON AND ALMONDS

Oaxaca, Mexico. I was sitting cross-legged on the ground in pale February sunshine watching 60-year-old Genoveva Martinez make chocolate the way her ancestors did. She knelt on a mat in front of a rectangular stone slab, a *metate*, and a flame sat underneath to keep it warm. Genoveva placed sticks of cinnamon and freshly roasted and peeled cacao beans on the *metate* and began grinding them with a long stone, her strong arms moving rhythmically and rapidly, the firm action of her wrists crushing the ingredients to a powder. She added more beans and continued grinding, until I noticed the powder give up its oil and transform into a paste the colour and sheen of a chestnut pony. Genoveva added sugar and ground walnuts to the slab and kept the action going, putting her back into her work and scraping down the *metate* now and again with a knife until the mixture released a heavenly scent. "It's ready when I can see my reflection; it shines like a mirror," Genoveva said. And suddenly the mixture was so much more than the sum of its parts: chocolate.

This laborious process has always been woven into the fabric of Genoveva's life. As a small child she would take it in turns with her sister to climb onto the backs of her mother's legs as she made chocolate this way, to enjoy the ride. As a young woman, Genoveva's suitability for being a wife was judged by her skills at the *metate*. "A girl couldn't marry until she learned to make chocolate," she said.

This is my version of Genoveva's hot chocolate. The mix keeps well in a sealed jar inside a cool cupboard.

MAKES ENOUGH FOR 6 CUPS
140g/5oz dark chocolate (around 70% cocoa solids), broken into pieces
1 tsp ground cinnamon
2 heaped tsp flaked [slivered] almonds
2½ Tbsp soft light brown sugar
good pinch of sea salt flakes

TO SERVE
whole milk
chilli flakes

Place all the ingredients for the chocolate mix in a food processor and blitz to a fine rubble—don't overdo it, or the chocolate will melt and turn into a paste.

Heat the milk in a pan almost to boiling point, then remove from the heat and add 3 tablespoons for each 250ml/8½fl oz of milk used. Whisk or beat to a lovely froth. Serve with a pinch of chilli flakes on top.

THICK AND SILKY SPANISH HOT CHOCOLATE WITH CINNAMON CREAM

As a child raised on Weetabix or porridge [oatmeal] for breakfast, I was dumbfounded to discover when I visited Spain for the first time that some Spaniards start the day with churros (doughnuts) dunked in thick hot chocolate. This recipe is authentically—and ridiculously—rich and intense, which is why the quantities per person are teeny. It's intended to be tinkered with according to your taste: use a pinch of ground aniseed or fennel seeds instead of star anise, or chilli flakes or paprika, if you like. Using water instead of milk is gloriously intense—but not for the fainthearted.

If you can't be doing with making churros in the morning—and frankly, who can?—whip up some hot buttered toast sprinkled with cinnamon and sugar, cut the toast into soldiers and dip into the chocolate instead.

SERVES 4 OR MAKES 600ML / 21FL OZ
30g/1oz cocoa powder
4 tsp cornflour [cornstarch]
pinch of sea salt flakes
500ml/17fl oz milk or water
50g/1¾oz granulated or caster [superfine] sugar
1 star anise
1 tsp vanilla extract

100g/3½oz dark chocolate (between 60–70% cocoa solids), grated

TO SERVE
ground cinnamon to taste (optional)
softly whipped cream (optional)

Combine the cocoa powder, cornflour and salt in a small bowl or cup.

Place the milk or water, sugar, star anise and vanilla in a small pan and almost bring to the boil, stirring until the sugar dissolves. Pour enough of the hot liquid into the cocoa powder mixture to make a paste and stir until smooth.

While the pan is off the heat, add the grated chocolate and cocoa paste to the milk. Stir until the chocolate has melted and everything is well combined. Return the pan to a low heat and stir until thick and creamy—use a whisk if you need to get rid of any lumps. Remove the star anise and discard. Add cinnamon to the whipped cream (if using) and serve a spoonful on top of the chocolate.

JASMINE-INFUSED MEDICI HOT CHOCOLATE

In Renaissance Italy, gluttonous Cosimo III de' Medici, Grand Duke of Tuscany, was known for hosting extravagant banquets for which he amassed rare and exotic ingredients from all over the globe, including chocolate. To please his patron, Cosimo's clever physician Francesco Redi invented novel ways to combine chocolate with perfumed flavours, such as musk, ambergris and citrus. But it was his jasmine-infused chocolate drink that became the speciality of Cosimo's court. Redi jealously guarded the recipe, which was only revealed after his death: vast quantities of fresh jasmine flowers were layered between cacao nibs and left for days to absorb the perfume of the blooms. Jasmine chocolate is still made this way by Pierpaolo Ruta of Antica Dolceria Bonajuto in Modica, Sicily. He uses 2,500 jasmine buds per 1kg [2lb 4oz] of nibs to create his seventeenth-century chocolate, which he sells in heavenly but dainty 1g morsels.

This recipe is a far less extravagant way to enjoy jasmine and chocolate, using tea instead of flowers. The same method can be used with other teas: the gentle spiciness of chai works well, as does smoky lapsang souchong and black tea—but as the latter two have robust flavours, I only use 1 teabag/tablespoon per serve.

SERVES 1 OR MAKES 250ML / 8½FL OZ
25g/1oz milk chocolate (between
   30–40% cocoa solids), grated or
   finely chopped
200ml/6¾fl oz whole milk
2 jasmine teabags or 2 scant Tbsp loose
   leaf jasmine tea

Place the chocolate in a mug. Pour the milk into a pan and bring almost to the boil. Remove from the heat and add the teabags or tea. Stir, then set aside for 3 minutes—don't leave it any longer or the infusion will be bitter, not floral. Remove the teabags or strain if using leaves. Pour over the chocolate and stir until melted. Serve immediately.

CACAO NIB INFUSIONS

Fresh and delicate but with an unmistakeable chocolate flavour, drinks made with cacao nibs are lighter alternatives to hot or iced chocolate made with milk and cream. Basically, you get the flavour of cocoa without the sugar and dairy.

To make cacao nib tea, steep 1 tablespoon nibs per person in just-boiled water for 5–10 minutes and strain before serving hot. Add flavours to the pot if you like: bay, mint, basil or lime leaves, a rosemary sprig, citrus peel (lime, lemon, orange and bergamot) or lavender sprigs all make delicious cacao nib brews.

Nibs also make refreshing cold drinks. Infuse 1 tablespoon nibs per person in just-boiled water as above, but steep them in a sealed jar or a jug covered in plastic wrap in the fridge for 24 hours. Serve strained over ice, with or without a splash of milk.

Whatever you do, don't discard the nibs once you have made your infusion. They'll be lovely and soft after seeping, and are perfect folded through ice cream or custard, added to cookie dough, cake batter, alcohol or even salad dressings.

You can also make an intense mocha drink by adding 1 tablespoon nibs per person to ground coffee in a French press, Aero press or filter.

CACAO-INFUSED TIPPLE

Alcohol infused with cacao nibs tastes fantastic, served straight over ice, or mixed into cocktails. You can use this recipe to infuse whatever tipple you fancy: vodka, tequila, bourbon, whisky and rum all work well.

MAKES 500ML / 17FL OZ
500ml/17fl oz alcohol of choice
50g/1¾oz cacao nibs
2 Tbsp coffee beans, lightly crushed
1 vanilla pod [bean]

Pour the alcohol of your choice into a stoppered bottle. Using a funnel, add the cacao nibs and crushed coffee beans. Poke the vanilla pod into the bottle, too. Leave to infuse for at least 2 weeks, shaking often, then strain through a fine mesh sieve [strainer] or coffee filter and return to the bottle. Seal and chill for up to 3 months.

MULLED COCOA WINE

This warming Christmassy brew is a terrific example of how cocoa can add subtle flavour and richness to food and drink without elbowing its way to the front of the pack and screaming out CHOCOLATE! I haven't specified the wine to use here, but go for something like a light and fruity Shiraz, a jammy Zinfandel, spicy Grenache or a Chilean Merlot. You don't need to spend a lot on something gorgeous, as you want a plain canvas for all the other flavours.

SERVES 2–4 (MAKES ABOUT 600ML / 21FL OZ)
6 Tbsp Cocoa Syrup (see page 66)
1 bottle fruity red wine
3 Tbsp Grand Marnier, brandy or port
6 cloves
6 cardamom pods, crushed with the side of a knife

2-cm / ¾-in piece of fresh ginger, peeled and sliced
1 cinnamon stick, broken in half
good grating of nutmeg
1 orange, halved and juiced, skins reserved, plus orange slices to serve (optional)

Start by making the Cocoa Syrup on page 66. You won't need it all but it will keep in a sealed jar in the fridge for a month or so.

Add the remaining ingredients to a pan, including the squeezed out orange skins, and stir in 6 tablespoons of the Cocoa Syrup. Simmer gently for 10 minutes, stirring now and then so the syrup is fully incorporated. Ladle the wine into heatproof glasses or mugs and serve warm with orange slices, if you like.

MARIE ANTOINETTE'S HOT CHOCOLATE ELIXIR
WITH ORANGE BLOSSOM AND ALMONDS

Someone who knew her chocolate was Marie Antoinette, reputedly one of the world's first chocoholics. She had her own master chocolate maker in tow when she arrived at Versailles in 1770 to start married life with King Louis XVI. He devised some delicious recipes to amuse his Queen, infusing her breakfast chocolate with fashionable ingredients such as orange blossom and almonds. To reflect the decadence of this hugely expensive drink, special tea sets were produced. One such set, made by master silversmith Jean-Pierre Charpenat, included over a hundred items, some ornamented with precious stones and ivory. On bathing mornings, the Queen was served a cup of chocolate in her slipper bath—a regime we might all aspire to. This refreshing recipe, informed by records of the Chateau of Versailles, should set you on your way to a regal hot chocolate experience.

SERVES 2 OR MAKES 300ML / 10FL OZ
200ml/6¾fl oz whole milk
finely grated zest and juice of 1 orange
60ml/2fl oz double [heavy] cream
½ tsp orange blossom water
pinch of salt

1 tsp caster [superfine] sugar
40g/1½oz dark chocolate (between
   60–70% cocoa solids), grated
toasted flaked [slivered] almonds,
   to serve (optional)

Place all the ingredients, except the chocolate and flaked almonds, in a small pan. Stir over a medium heat until the sugar has dissolved and the mixture is hot but not boiling.

Remove the pan from the heat, add the chocolate and stir until melted. Return the pan to a medium-low heat and whisk with a balloon whisk until creamy and slightly thickened with a lovely froth. Serve topped with flaked almonds, and consume reclining in a bath scented with orange blossoms.

CHOCOLATE PRALINE PECAN SAUCE

One of the reasons I love this sauce so much is that you can gussy it up according to your mood or the occasion. I sometimes add a handful of dried cranberries, sour cherries or even barberries at the same time as the chocolate for a lovely tart contrast to the sweetness. Of course, it's divine with a splosh of alcohol—just add it to the caramel sauce. Kirsch works beautifully if you're adding sour cherries, but you won't regret sploshing brandy, sherry or bourbon into the mix. For my taste, about 2 tablespoons is about right, but each to their own.

MAKES 350ML / 12FL OZ OR SERVES 6

50g/1¾oz pecan nuts
180ml/6fl oz evaporated milk
140g/5oz light muscovado [brown] sugar
2 Tbsp unsalted butter
1 tsp vanilla extract
generous pinch of sea salt flakes,
   plus extra to taste
100g/3½oz dark chocolate
   (70% cocoa solids), grated or
   finely chopped

Spread the pecans in a single layer in a dry frying pan and cook over a medium-high heat, stirring frequently, until they smell toasty and they've browned a little at the edges. Roughly chop, making sure to leave some big bits.

Place the evaporated milk, sugar, butter, vanilla and salt in a medium pan (and the alcohol, if using) and cook over a gentle heat, stirring all the time, until the sugar is dissolved and everything is amalgamated. Increase the heat and simmer until the caramel thickens slightly.

Remove the pan from the heat and stir the chocolate (and dried fruit if using) into the hot caramel until completely amalgamated, smooth and glossy. Fold in the pecans. When the sauce is cool enough, have a taste and add more salt if needed. Serve warm or cool.

Chocolate and malt have been contented bedfellows since the 1930s when the late Forrest Mars Sr. — the man who built the Mars confectionery empire — launched Maltesers in the UK. He originally marketed the chocolate-coated malted bites as 'energy balls' and aimed them squarely at women who were trying to lose weight. He argued that because the centres were light and airy, they were less fattening than solid chocolate. Maltesers went on to become the best-selling chocolate brand in the UK; they were only launched in the US in 2017 after a protracted legal wrangle between Mars and Hershey, which sold a rival malted-milk snack. This scrumptious malted chocolate sauce is like a liquid version of those famous sweets [candies] and uses rich and gloopy malt extract — a much underused syrup made from sprouted barley grains, and available in health food shops. For an adult version, a splosh or two of whisky continues the malt theme most deliciously.

MAKES ABOUT 175ML / 6FL OZ
OR SERVES 4

85g/3oz dark chocolate (between 60–70% cocoa solids), grated or finely chopped
80ml/2¾fl oz double [heavy] cream
70ml/2½fl oz malt extract (available from health food shops)
2½ Tbsp soft dark brown sugar
2 Tbsp unsalted butter
splash or two of whisky (optional)
generous pinch of sea salt flakes
vanilla ice cream, to serve

Place the chocolate in a heatproof bowl.

Place the cream, malt extract, sugar, butter, whisky (if using) and salt in a pan and cook over a medium heat until everything melts together. Pour the hot cream over the chocolate, stirring constantly, until you have a voluptuous sauce, whisking if needed to remove any lumps. This is glorious served warm over vanilla ice cream.

Clockwise from back: Chocolate Praline Pecan Sauce; Malted Chocolate Fudge Sauce; Salted Caramel and Lime Chocolate Sauce

SALTED CARAMEL AND LIME CHOCOLATE SAUCE

As Niki Segnit says in her endlessly useful book, *The Flavour Thesaurus*, lime and chocolate is a delicious combination that rarely crops up in forms other than chocolate limes, the classic British sweet. This recipe redresses this sad situation: it's a tongue-tingling sauce that works beautifully with vanilla ice cream.

MAKES ABOUT 250ML / 8½FL OZ
OR SERVES 4
120g/4¼oz soft light brown sugar
90ml/3fl oz lime juice
90ml/3fl oz double [heavy] cream

80g/2¾oz dark chocolate (between 60–70% cocoa solids), grated or finely chopped
good pinch of sea salt flakes
1 tsp unsalted butter

Place the sugar and lime juice in a heavy pan off the heat. Stir to combine and partly dissolve the sugar. Set over a medium-high heat and let the mixture bubble away until it turns dark amber and slightly syrupy: be careful not to let it burn. Remove the pan from the heat and stir in the cream—be careful as it will splatter —then stir in the chocolate, salt and butter to make a glossy sauce. Serve warm.

COCOA SYRUP

The moments it takes to conjure a batch of this intense syrup are time well spent. Drizzled into milkshakes, swirled over ice cream or cooked fruit, squirted into coffee or smuggled into a cocktail… it's worth having a jar on hand. You could add sage or rosemary to the syrup and strain before adding the cocoa; or anoint with a few drops of peppermint, orange or basil oil or a splosh of booze or vanilla extract.

MAKES ABOUT 300ML / 10FL OZ
240g/8½oz caster [superfine] sugar
240ml/8fl oz water
80g/2¾oz cocoa powder
generous pinch of sea salt flakes

Place the sugar and water in a small pan and stir over a medium heat until the sugar dissolves. Increase the heat and bubble away gently for 1 minute.

Place the cocoa and salt in a small mixing bowl and pour in just enough of the sugar mixture, stirring as you go, to make a smooth paste. Add the remaining sugar mixture, stirring, until glossy. Store in a sealed jar or bottle in the fridge for about a month. Gently reheat to make the syrup pourable again after chilling.

CHOCOLATE PORRIDGE WITH NIBS AND MARMALADE

At first glance, this might appear like a very decadent dessert-pretending-to-be-breakfast affair, but actually it's not. The cocoa, nibs and marmalade are bitter but deeply flavourful—and perfect counterpoints to the soothing creaminess of the tender oatmeal and grains. Add maple syrup to taste, or none if you prefer, as the marmalade and fruit will impart gentle sweetness.

SERVES 2

FOR THE PORRIDGE
60g/2¼oz porridge oats
60g/2¼oz rye, quinoa, buckwheat
  or rice flakes
2 Tbsp cacao nibs
4 Tbsp cocoa powder
250ml/8¾fl oz whole milk
250ml/8¾fl oz water
2 Tbsp maple syrup, or to taste (optional)
generous pinch of salt

TO SERVE
marmalade
orange segments (blood
  orange is delicious)
mixed seeds

Place all the porridge ingredients in a medium pan and stir well. Bring the mixture to the boil, then reduce the heat and simmer gently for 5 minutes or so, stirring frequently, until the grains are tender and the mixture is lovely and creamy.

Serve topped with a generous spoonful of marmalade, orange segments and a scattering of seeds.

HONEYED BREAKFAST POLENTA WITH
PLUM, BLACKBERRY AND NIB COMPOTE

In this warming and tasty breakfast bowl, the cacao nibs impart subtle chocolate notes that chime beautifully with the sweet and earthy flavour of the cornmeal. (Try to avoid buying instant or express cornmeal, as the flavour doesn't compare to the coarse stuff.) The nibs also provide pleasing pops of bitterness and a little firm but chewy texture.

SERVES 2

FOR THE COMPOTE
½ tsp fennel seeds
2 ripe plums, stones [pits] removed
  and chopped
100g/3½oz blackberries
2 Tbsp caster [superfine] sugar,
  or to taste
seeds from ½ vanilla pod [bean]
  or ½ tsp vanilla extract
squeeze of orange or lemon juice,
  plus extra if needed
2 Tbsp cacao nibs

FOR THE POLENTA
100ml/3½fl oz whole milk
pinch of salt
1 Tbsp grated orange zest
300ml/10fl oz water
75g/2¾oz coarse white or
  yellow cornmeal
1 Tbsp runny honey, or more to taste
1 Tbsp unsalted butter
demerara [light brown] sugar,
  for sprinkling

Start with the compote. Lightly toast the fennel seeds in a dry frying pan until fragrant, then blitz to a powder in a spice or coffee grinder or crush with a mortar and pestle. Place all the compote ingredients, including the ground fennel seeds, in a pan set over a medium heat. Stir while the plums and blackberries release their juices. Reduce the heat to low, squash the fruit down with the back of a spoon and let the mixture bubble away until the fruit is very soft and falling apart. Add a splash of water or orange juice if the compote becomes too thick or dry. Taste and add more sugar, if you like. Keep the pan half-on, half-off a low heat to keep warm.

Now make the polenta. Place the milk, salt, orange zest and water in a pan and bring to the boil. Slowly pour the cornmeal into the liquid in a thin stream, whisking all the time, until the mixture thickens.

Reduce the heat to low and cook for 30–40 minutes, stirring every 5 minutes or so, until creamy and tender. Add more water as necessary to produce the consistency that you find lovely. Remove the pan from the heat and stir in the honey and butter. Serve immediately with the compote spooned over the top and a sprinkling of demerara sugar.

COCOA: A CUP BEFORE BEDTIME

"So let any man who has drunk too deeply of the cup of pleasure, or given to work a notable portion of the time which should belong to sleep; who finds his wit temporarily losing its edge, the atmosphere humid, time dragging, the air hard to breathe, or who is tortured by a fixed idea which robs him of all freedom of thought; let such a man administer to himself a good pint of ambered chocolate... and he will see wonders." —Jean Anthelme Brillat-Savarin, *The Pleasures of the Table*

As a child growing up in Australia, hot chocolate meant one thing only: Milo. A couple of teaspoons of the wondrous malted-chocolate granules (more if you could sneak them past the adults) stirred into hot milk was nirvana in a mug. As Milo aficionados know, only some of the granules dissolve, the rest rise to the top to form a crunchy chocolate layer that's luscious to devour with a spoon. (Milo's inventor Thomas Mayne is said to have toiled hard to crack the problem of the non-dissolving granules until his children begged him not to bother). Developed by Mayne for Nestlé in 1934 to fortify the diets of undernourished children in the aftermath of the Depression, Milo, in its iconic green tin, remains a stalwart of the nation's kitchen cupboards and is still marketed as a nutritious 'food drink'.

Although I'll love Milo until I draw my last breath, I had a hot chocolate epiphany in the French Alps years later, when I tasted the proper stuff for the very first time. It was a revelation. Thick, rich, velvety and dark as midnight — made with real chocolate, not granules or powder, and topped with a billow of Chantilly cream — that steaming mugful was the sweetest revenge against the cold and my failed attempts to learn to ski.

And that's why hot chocolate is one of life's great joys. More extrovert than tea, more sensual than coffee, it warms body and soul with sweet energy and flavour, reviving and cheering when life gets us down. Preparing a decadent mugful—perhaps pimped with spices or a splosh of alcohol—can be a valuable act of kindness to yourself and improve a bad day immeasurably.

Intriguingly, hot chocolate has always been valued this way. When the ancients first unlocked the secrets of how to turn the bitter beans of the cacao pod into a drink, they regarded it as magical, a gift from the Gods. Certainly, making chocolate was deemed to be worth the considerable effort involved. Women—and it was only women who performed the arduous task—worked on their knees to grind the cacao beans with a pestle (*mano*) on a hot stone slab (*metate*). They mixed the resulting aromatic paste with water and flavourings, such as chilli, vanilla and Amazonian 'ear flowers' —sometimes honey to sweeten—and poured the drink from one vessel to another from a height to produce a highly prized foam.

The Mayans and later the Aztecs—who eagerly embraced cacao when they conquered large parts of Mexico in the late fourteenth century—drank chocolate for religious reasons and on ceremonial occasions. A cup of chocolate sealed marriage vows, nourished women before and after childbirth, sustained labourers, energized soldiers, and was the highlight of extravagant feasts. But it was also valued for its medicinal properties, sometimes mixed with other healing plants to treat a range of ailments, from stomach complaints to coughs. And, of course, its stimulating effects were highly prized. The Aztec emperor Montezuma was reported to have guzzled many golden goblets of spiced chocolate in one sitting, 'for success with women' according to the account of one Spanish observer. The story helped shape chocolate's reputation as an aphrodisiac, although its stimulating powers were more likely due to the drink being alcoholic as a result of the fermentation process.

The Conquistadors, who vanquished the Aztecs in the sixteenth century, weren't initially convinced; to their unaccustomed palates, chocolate tasted repulsively bitter. But when cacao beans eventually arrived in Spain, Charles I and the royal court quickly modified chocolate to their own taste, consuming it warm (unlike the Aztecs, who liked theirs cold), sweetened with sugar cane and flavoured with more familiar and readily available aromatics such as rose petals or rose oil from the Middle East, anise, cinnamon and black pepper. Perhaps to emulate the style of New World chocolate drinks that were often thickened with maize, the Spanish sometimes added almonds, eggs or milk to their chocolate drinks.

Hot chocolate quickly became fashionable throughout Catholic Spain, at least among those who could afford it, for both chocolate and sugar were expensive luxury imports. One theory for why this happened is that the Catholic Church in Spain eventually allowed chocolate to be consumed on religious fast days. Perhaps this was thanks to the support of the religious orders who, in the early days of chocolate in Europe, were responsible for roasting and grinding cacao beans, and shaped them into the tablets that the great and the good dissolved in water or milk for their drinks.

For many years, hot chocolate remained Spain's gastronomical secret, but word eventually spread to France. One theory is that the Spanish Infanta Maria Theresa introduced chocolate to King Louis XIV when she married him in 1660, propelling the drink into French high society. From there, hot chocolate spread inexorably to the grand houses and palaces of Baroque Europe, where the aristocracy revelled in consuming an exotic drink beyond the financial means of most.

The elite soon required suitably prestigious accoutrements to prepare and consume the exalted drink. Chocolate pots were crafted in silver and porcelain, with holes in the centre of the lid to hold a *molinillo,* or whisking stick, for creating froth. Deep saucers with a collar-like ring in the middle were devised to prevent unseemly chocolate spillage, particularly useful for ladies taking their breakfast chocolate in bed. Known as *mancerinas* in Spain and *trembleuses* in France, exquisite porcelain versions were crafted by the great potters of Europe, along with matching cups, sometimes with lids, to keep the chocolate warm.

Hot chocolate arrived in London around 1657, only a few years after coffee, via an entrepreneurial Frenchman who sold the 'excellent West India drink' ready made and in coarse tablets for customers to grate or break into pieces and dissolve in hot water at home. Expensive and wildly different to any other drink before, chocolate was heavily marketed as medicinal to encourage consumers to try it. The noted diarist Samuel Pepys, who was among the first in England to drink chocolate, needed no convincing. He praised the beverage as a hangover cure that relieved his 'sad head' and 'imbecilic stomach'.

Special Chocolate Kitchens were installed at Hampton Court Palace in around 1690, by William III and Queen Mary II, so that royal chocolate makers could prepare the uber-fashionable and expensive — but messy to prepare — drink from scratch. Cacao beans were roasted, flavoured and ground on a hot stone *metate* (just as they were in the New World) to form a paste, which was shaped into blocks and left to mature for several months. The cakes were melted into drinks made with hot milk, water or wine, and then sweetened with sugar and flavoured with spices.

The drink was taken from the Chocolate Kitchen to the high-security Chocolate Room, where expensive gilded chocolate pots and porcelain cups were stored. The chocolate was then poured into these elaborate serving vessels and taken to the king or queen, who usually enjoyed it at breakfast time. William, however, was partial to hot chocolate throughout the day.

Hot chocolate slowly filtered down the social classes during the seventeenth and eighteenth centuries, via the coffee houses and chocolate parlours that sprang up across Europe. In the super-elite area around London's St James's Square, near Piccadilly, chocolate parlours flourished, eventually evolving into gentlemen's clubs. White's and the Cocoa Tree were among the most infamous, known for the debauched behaviour of patrons who gambled their money away and debated the hot political topics of the day over cups of chocolate, coffee and alcohol. Jonathan Swift famously lamented White's as 'the most fashionable hell in London', while King Charles II tried — and failed — to have it closed down.

It was not until the first half of the nineteenth century, when Dutchman Coenraad van Houten invented the press that made cocoa powder possible, that hot chocolate became a drink accessible to the masses. In 1866, the Cadbury brothers introduced van Houten's technology to their Birmingham factory, which revolutionized British cocoa making. Until this time, chocolate had been heavily adulterated with starches such as potato flour or sago to mask the cocoa butter; George Cadbury himself described these drinks as 'comforting gruel'. But using the new press, Cadbury was able to produce a more palatable 'pure' cocoa essence — the forerunner of the cocoa powder we know today.

Hot chocolate was soon bolstering the diets of the military. In the late eighteenth century, the British government allocated seamen in the Royal Navy a ration of drinking chocolate as an alternative to rum. During the American Civil War, medics administered chocolate to wounded and poorly soldiers to aid their recovery. Thomas Jefferson was so impressed with the drink he predicted, "The superiority of chocolate, both for health and nourishment, will soon give it the preference over tea and coffee in America." He might have missed the mark slightly, but the development of easy to make, transportable chocolate powder paved the way for hot chocolate to become a valuable source of sustenance for soldiers on battlefields in major conflicts. During World War II, for example, the piping hot mugs of cocoa served by YMCA volunteers were hailed as 'a welcome tonic' for weary soldiers. Cocoa powder or drinking chocolate remains a staple in many military ration packs today.

Hot, filling and rejuvenating, hot chocolate has also featured in major expeditions to the North and South Poles. Captain Robert Falcon Scott and his crew reached the South Pole on 17 January 1912 after travelling for over a year on a diet that consisted largely of hot chocolate and stew. Even though chocolate's sustaining powers were, ultimately, insufficient for the team's physical exertions, Scott said that mugs of cocoa mixed with sugar prevented the men from wanting to kill each other.

Many aficionados bemoan the demise of 'real hot chocolate' and the rise of powdered chocolate drinks where cocoa is bulked out with sugar, vegetable fats, powdered milk, thickeners and artificial flavourings. But, in line with the rise of the fine chocolate movement, a new generation of chocolate houses is emerging, serving exquisite concoctions made from quality bars, imbued with flavours that even the Mayans might recognize, such as chilli and vanilla. It's a welcome development for hot chocolate lovers like me, even though there will always be a place in my cupboard—and my heart—for Milo.

SOMETHING TO SLICE

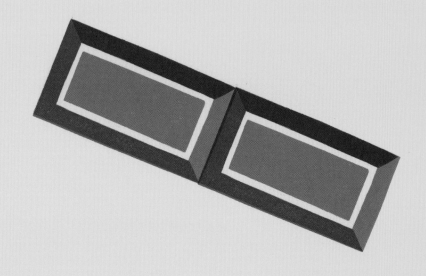

ARABIAN NIGHTS COFFEE CHOCOLATE LAYER CAKE WITH ROSE-SCENTED GANACHE

It's a bit of a mystery why chocolate didn't really conquer the Middle East the same way it did Europe in the early days. One theory is that coffee was already a much-loved beverage in those lands by the time the cacao bean arrived in Venice, the gateway to the Middle East. Less expensive than cocoa and with a bigger caffeine hit, coffee effectively stymied the march of drinking chocolate. And of course, the hot Middle Eastern climate was not conducive to the production of eating chocolate. Whatever the reason, the flavours of the Middle East work gorgeously with cocoa: here I wanted to combine cardamom-infused Turkish coffee and the flavours of Turkish delight in an intense chocolate cake. I think the result is delicious.

SERVES 8–12

90g/3¼oz unsalted butter, plus extra
  for greasing
250g/8¾oz plain [all-purpose] flour
1½ tsp bicarbonate of soda [baking soda]
½ tsp fine sea salt
½ tsp finely ground cardamom seeds
200g/7oz dark chocolate (between
  70–75% cocoa solids), grated or blitzed
  in a food processor
120ml/4fl oz vegetable oil
400g/14oz caster [superfine] sugar
4 large eggs, lightly beaten
2 tsp vanilla extract
240ml/8fl oz strong hot espresso

FOR THE GANACHE

200g/7oz dark chocolate (70% cocoa
  solids), chopped
250ml/8½fl oz double [heavy] cream
20g/¾oz caster [superfine] sugar
½ tsp rosewater

FOR THE COFFEE BUTTERCREAM

150g/5¼oz soft unsalted butter, softened
300g/10½oz icing [confectioners']
  sugar, sifted
1 Tbsp instant coffee granules dissolved
  in 1 Tbsp boiling water

TO DECORATE (OPTIONAL)

edible rose petals and/or crystallized
  [candied] rose petals

Preheat the oven to 180°C/350°F/Gas mark 4. Butter 2 × 20-cm/8-in round cake tins and line the bases with baking paper.

Using a fork or balloon whisk, whisk the flour, bicarbonate of soda, salt and cardamom seeds together in a bowl to combine and set aside.

Melt the chocolate, butter and oil together in a heatproof bowl set over a pan of barely simmering water, making sure the bottom of the bowl doesn't touch the water. Stir to combine, then remove the pan from the heat.

Place the caster sugar in a mixing bowl or the bowl of a stand mixer, add the melted chocolate mixture and beat until well combined — it might turn a little grainy, but that's fine. Gradually beat in the eggs and vanilla to produce a smooth shiny batter. Beat in the flour mixture on low speed until just combined. Finally, beat in the hot coffee, giving a final stir with a spatula to make sure all the melted chocolate at the bottom of the bowl is mixed in.

Divide the batter evenly between the prepared cake tins and bake for about 35 minutes — but start checking after 30 minutes — until a skewer inserted into the centre comes out clean. Leave in the tins for 5 minutes, then turn out onto a wire rack to cool completely.

To make the ganache, place the chocolate in a heatproof mixing bowl. Heat the cream and caster sugar together in a small pan until almost boiling and the sugar has dissolved, stirring all the while so it doesn't catch. Stir in the rosewater, then immediately pour over the chocolate, stirring constantly until all the chocolate has melted. Leave to cool for 5 minutes, then whisk with a balloon whisk or electric beaters until thick and creamy. This can take a few minutes.

To make the coffee buttercream, beat the butter in a stand mixer or in a bowl with electric beaters until very pale and creamy, then add the icing sugar and coffee and beat until creamy.

To assemble, carefully cut each cake in half horizontally with a serrated knife. Spread the tops of 3 of the cakes with buttercream, then set one on top of the other. Place the un-iced cake on top with its neatest side facing upwards.

Finish by spreading the ganache over the top and sides — smoothly or in swirls, as you wish. It should spread very easily, so if it has hardened too much, beat well or melt a little over a pan of barely simmering water. Decorate with edible and/or crystallized rose petals, if using.

PISTACHIO AND NUTMEG CAKE WITH CHOCOLATE AND RASPBERRIES

Chocolate cakes don't have to be insanely rich and intensely chocolaty. There's nothing wrong with those attributes, of course, but sometimes just a touch of chocolate is in order. This is it: a cake that's decadent, but gently so, with the flavour of the nutmeg bringing out the cocoa notes of the milk chocolate, and tangy raspberries a foil to the sweetness. Adorned with berries, nuts and edible flowers, this is perfect for an elegant summer's afternoon tea.

SERVES 8

120g/4¼oz unsalted butter, at room
   temperature, plus extra for greasing
100g/3½oz shelled pistachios,
   plus extra to decorate
270g/9½oz plain [all-purpose] flour
4 Tbsp cornflour [cornstarch]
2 tsp baking powder
¾ tsp bicarbonate of soda [baking soda]
1½ tsp grated nutmeg
¼ tsp fine sea salt
270g/9½oz caster [superfine] sugar
2 whole large eggs, lightly beaten
2 tsp vanilla extract
150ml/5fl oz milk
100ml/3½fl oz water
3 large egg whites
edible flowers, to decorate

FOR THE CHOCOLATE GANACHE

200g/7oz milk chocolate (at least
   30% cocoa solids), chopped small
100ml/3½fl oz double [heavy] cream
pinch of sea salt flakes

FOR THE MASCARPONE CREAM

120g/4¼oz mascarpone cheese
120g/4¼oz crème fraîche
1½ Tbsp icing [confectioners'] sugar,
   plus extra to taste
150–200g/5¼–7oz raspberries

Preheat the oven to 160°C/325°F/Gas mark 3. Butter 2 × 20-cm/8-in round cake tins and line the bases with baking paper.

Blitz the pistachios in a spice or coffee grinder until fine, being careful not to reduce to a paste. (A food processor won't get them fine enough for the best results, but don't worry if that's what you have—the cake will just be a little heavier.) Transfer to a mixing bowl, add both flours, the baking powder, bicarbonate of soda, nutmeg and salt and, using a fork or balloon whisk, whisk to combine. Set aside.

Beat the butter and sugar together in a stand mixer or in a bowl with electric beaters until very pale and fluffy—this will take a good 5 minutes. Gradually beat in the whole eggs and vanilla, then beat for a few minutes more.

With the machine on a low speed, beat in the flour mixture in several separate additions, alternating with the milk and water, until just incorporated.

In a scrupulously clean bowl, whisk the egg whites to soft peaks, then gently fold them into the batter.

Divide the batter equally between the prepared tins and smooth the tops. Bake for 35–40 minutes until golden and a skewer inserted into the centre of the cakes comes out clean. Leave to cool in the tins for 5 minutes, then turn out onto a wire rack to cool completely.

To make the ganache, place the chocolate in a heatproof bowl. Gently heat the cream until hot but not boiling, then pour over the chocolate. Add the salt and stir until melted and gorgeously thick and shiny. Leave to cool.

For the mascarpone cream, in a stand mixer or in a bowl with electric beaters, beat the mascarpone, crème fraîche and icing sugar together until smooth. Squash 50g/1¾oz of the raspberries with a fork and gently fold through the mascarpone cream.

To assemble the cake, spread the tops of both cooled cakes with the ganache, then spread one of the cakes with the mascarpone cream and place the other cake on top, chocolate-side upwards. Decorate the top with the remaining raspberries, pistachios and the edible flowers. Serve immediately.

CHOCOLATE, LAVENDER AND LEMON BUNDT CAKE

The combination of chocolate, lavender and lemon is an absolute winner in this cake. The lavender is subtle—I promise you it's not like nibbling a bar of Grandma's soap at all—and the lemon adds freshness to the whole shebang. The cake itself is light and moist, but one best eaten within a couple of days.

SERVES 8-10

vegetable oil, for oiling
¾ Tbsp culinary lavender buds (see note)
350g/12¼oz caster [superfine] sugar
200g/7oz unsalted butter, softened
280g/10oz plain [all-purpose] flour
50g/1¾oz dark chocolate (between
  60–70% cocoa solids), grated
50g/1¾oz cocoa powder
1 tsp baking powder
½ tsp bicarbonate of soda [baking soda]
½ tsp fine sea salt
3 large eggs
180g/6½oz Greek yogurt
1–2 Tbsp milk

FOR THE GLAZE

200g/7oz icing [confectioners'] sugar
40–50ml/1⅓–1⅔fl oz lemon juice
1½ Tbsp unsalted butter, melted
pinch of salt
lavender sprigs, to decorate

Preheat the oven to 170°C/340°F/Gas mark 3. Generously brush the inside of a 2.4-litre/81-fl oz/2.5-quart Bundt tin with oil, making sure to get into all the crevices.

Blitz the lavender and half the sugar to a powder in a food processor. Transfer to a mixing bowl or the bowl of a stand mixer, add the remaining sugar and the butter and beat until very pale and creamy—this will take at least 7 minutes.

Using a fork or balloon whisk, whisk the flour, grated chocolate, cocoa, baking powder, bicarbonate of soda and salt together in another bowl.

In a small jug, whisk the eggs and yogurt together. Add this to the butter and sugar mixture, alternating with the flour mixture, beating well after each addition. Add a splash of milk to loosen if the batter is too stiff to fall off the end of a wooden spoon, but it shouldn't be runny.

Spoon the batter into the prepared tin, smoothing with the back of a spoon to ensure that the batter fills all the crevices at the bottom of the tin. Tap the tin on the work surface a couple of times to remove all the air bubbles. Bake for 40–45 minutes until a skewer inserted in the centre of the cake comes out clean. Leave to cool in the tin for 15 minutes, then turn out onto a wire rack to cool.

To make the glaze, mix the icing sugar, lemon juice, melted butter and salt together in a bowl. Drizzle over the cooled cake so that it covers the top and runs down the sides, then decorate with lavender sprigs.

Note: Culinary lavender is a particularly flavourful variety sold in speciality shops specifically to cook with. Unsprayed lavender buds from the garden are fine but might vary in strength.

STICKY TOFFEE PUDDING CAKE WITH
CHOCOLATE, SALTED CARAMEL AND NIB BRITTLE

This is a real celebratory confection and unapologetically sweet, just like its namesake, sticky toffee pudding. A hugely popular 'British' pudding, it's widely claimed to have been invented in England's Lake District in the 1970s, although British food writer Felicity Cloake says there's evidence it originated in Canada. Whatever its provenance, the original contained no chocolate, but cocoa flavours work beautifully with the notes of caramel and toffee in the brown sugar. Serve small slices by all means, but I've lost count of the times a guest has remarked on its sweetness as they simultaneously help themselves to a second or third slice. It's that kind of cake.

SERVES 8

200g/7oz fresh pitted dates
1¼ tsp bicarbonate of soda [baking soda]
300ml/10fl oz freshly boiled water
75g/2¾oz unsalted butter
60g/2¼oz soft light brown sugar
60g/2¼oz soft dark brown sugar
2 large eggs, lightly beaten
200g/7oz plain [all-purpose] flour
1½ tsp baking powder
pinch of salt
100g/3½oz dark chocolate (between
    70–85% cocoa solids), roughly chopped,
    or chocolate chips

FOR THE SALTED CARAMEL BUTTERCREAM

80ml/2¾fl oz double [heavy] cream
125g/4½oz caster [superfine] sugar
4 Tbsp water
200g/7oz unsalted butter
2 tsp sea salt flakes
240g/8½oz icing [confectioners'] sugar

FOR THE NIB BRITTLE

45g/1½oz caster [superfine] sugar
2 Tbsp water
2 Tbsp cacao nibs

Preheat the oven to 180°C/350°F/Gas mark 4. Line the base of a 20-cm/8-in round cake tin with baking paper.

Chop the dates into large pieces—I like quite big chunks so I generally just cut each one in half. Place in a heatproof bowl and sprinkle over the bicarbonate of soda. Add the freshly boiled water, making sure the dates are submerged and set aside.

Beat the butter and both sugars together in a stand mixer or in a bowl with electric beaters until creamy. Gradually add the eggs, beating well between each addition, adding a spoonful of flour if the mixture curdles.

Using a fork or balloon whisk, whisk the flour, baking powder and salt together in a bowl and set aside.

Pour the dates and their soaking water through a sieve [strainer] into a jug, reserving the liquid. Add the dates to the butter, sugar and egg mixture and beat on low speed until just combined.

Measure out 200ml/6¾fl oz of the date soaking water (discard the rest) and add to the batter in several additions, alternating with scoops of the flour mixture until both are used up. You should have a loose but not runny batter. Fold in the chocolate.

Pour the batter into the prepared tin and smooth the top. Bake for 40 minutes, or until risen, firm to touch on top and a skewer inserted into the centre of the cake comes out clean of batter, although it will be chocolaty. Leave in the tin for 10 minutes, then turn out onto a wire rack to cool.

Meanwhile, make the buttercream. Make sure you have the cream measured out before you start. Place the caster sugar and water in a heavy, light-coloured pan and stir to combine. Set the pan over a medium-high heat and let the sugar bubble away, swirling the pan occasionally (don't stir), until it turns a rich amber colour. Remove the pan from the heat and carefully pour in the cream, stirring as you go. Take care as the caramel will splutter. Stir until smooth, then scrape into a heatproof bowl to cool completely.

While the caramel is cooling, make the brittle. Line a baking sheet with baking paper and have the nibs ready by the hob [stove]. Rinse out the pan you used to make the caramel, add the sugar and water and stir to combine. Let the mixture bubble away over a medium-high heat, swirling the pan occasionally, until it's a rich amber colour. Remove the pan from the heat and quickly stir in the nibs. Return the pan to the heat for a few seconds, stirring constantly. Pour the mixture onto the prepared baking sheet and spread out with the back of a spoon to make a thin layer. Leave for about 5–10 minutes to cool and set.

Once the caramel for the buttercream has cooled, beat the butter and salt together until creamy. Gradually beat in the icing [confectioners'] sugar, then add the cooled caramel and beat until fluffy.

To assemble, cut the cooled cake in half horizontally with a serrated knife. Spread some of the buttercream over the cut side of one half and place the other half on top. Slather the remaining buttercream over the top and sides of the cake — smoothly or in swirls, as you prefer. Chop up the brittle — it's nice to have a mixture of small and large pieces — and scatter over the top. Serve immediately.

CHOCOLATE MILK CAKE WITH PECAN PRALINE CREAM

Tres Leches Cake (Three Milks Cake) is thought to hail from Latin America—Mexico and several other countries lay claim to it. So-called because three types of milk—condensed milk, evaporated milk and cream—are poured over a plain sponge cake, it is, let's say, indulgent. I've adapted this recipe from one I stumbled across on the internet by chef Pablo Jacinto at Cindy's Backstreet Kitchen in St Helena, California. The meringue in the batter makes the sponge celestially light and fluffy: I've added cocoa to the soaking milks and—because more is more with a cake like this—spiked the whipped cream topping with pecan praline, which adds a welcome crunch and slightly burnt notes. Even if you're not a cream cake kind of person—I'm generally not—I love this one. It's a winner.

SERVES 12
butter, for greasing
200g/7oz plain [all-purpose] flour
1½ tsp baking powder
pinch of salt
5 large eggs, separated
280g/10oz caster [superfine] sugar
1½ tsp vanilla extract
70ml/2⅓fl oz milk

FOR THE CHOCOLATE MILK
200ml/6¾fl oz evaporated milk
200ml/6¾fl oz condensed milk
150ml/5fl oz double [heavy] cream
4 Tbsp cocoa powder

FOR THE PRALINE CREAM
150g/5¼oz caster [superfine] sugar
180ml/6fl oz water
100g/3½oz pecans, chopped small
450ml/15¼fl oz double [heavy] cream
½ tsp ground cinnamon

Preheat the oven to 180°C/350°F/Gas mark 4. Butter a 20×25-cm/8×9¾-in roasting tray (it needs to be at least 5cm/2in deep as the cake rises a lot).

Using a fork or balloon whisk, whisk the flour, baking powder and salt together in a bowl and set aside.

Whisk the egg whites in a stand mixer or in a bowl with electric beaters to soft peaks, then gradually whisk in the sugar to make a thick and glossy meringue. Whisk in the egg yolks, one at a time, and then the vanilla.

Sift one-quarter of the flour mixture over the meringue and gently fold it in with a metal spoon. Fold in one-quarter of the milk. Repeat until the flour and milk are used up. Don't rush this bit, as you want to retain as much of the air as possible. When the flour and milk are amalgamated, pour into the prepared tray, smooth the top and tap against the work surface a couple of times to remove any big air bubbles. Bake for 30–35 minutes until risen and golden, and a skewer inserted into the centre comes out clean. Leave in the tray to cool for 10 minutes.

While the cake is cooling, using a fork or balloon whisk, whisk all the chocolate milk ingredients together in a jug.

Run a knife between the edge of the cake and the tin and turn out onto a chopping board. Place a rimmed baking sheet on top of the cake and invert, so that it's right side up. Poke lots of holes in the top with a chopstick or skewer.

Pour a cupful of the chocolate milk mixture over the top of the cake and let it sink in; use a spoon to encourage it into the holes. Once it has absorbed, pour over more of the chocolate milk and continue until it's all used up. Cover with plastic wrap and chill for a few hours, ideally overnight, as this will allow the chocolate milk to seep right into the cake.

Meanwhile, make the pecan praline cream. Line a baking sheet with baking paper. In a small heavy pan, stir the sugar and water together. Let the mixture bubble away until it turns a pale amber. Add the pecans and stir to coat in the caramel. Continue cooking, stirring now and then, until the caramel turns deep amber. Quickly pour onto the prepared baking sheet and spread out to a thin layer, then leave for 30 minutes to harden. Once hard, roughly chop.

Whip the cream to soft peaks in a stand mixer, then fold in two-thirds of the pecan praline and the cinnamon. Slather the top of the cake with the cream and transfer to the fridge until ready to serve. Scatter with the remaining praline just before slicing.

CHOCOLATE GINGERBREAD CAKE WITH TONKA BEAN FROSTING

Fresh ginger is gorgeously complex, with flavour notes ranging from woody and earthy to citrusy and spicy—and it also delivers a lovely thwack of heat. Dark chocolate can echo ginger's flavour notes, which makes parking them both in the same dish so edifying. (Let the trumpets sound for chocolate-dipped crystallized ginger!) If you can't find tonka beans for the frosting—they're widely available in most countries online—substitute with the seeds scraped from a vanilla pod [bean].

SERVES 8-10

100g/3½oz unsalted butter,
  plus extra for greasing
80g/2¾oz golden [corn] syrup
100g/3½oz treacle [molasses]
100g/3½oz dark muscovado
  [brown] sugar
3 Tbsp syrup from a jar of stem
  [preserved] ginger
1 heaped Tbsp freshly grated ginger
180g/6oz plain [all-purpose] flour
30g/1oz cocoa powder
¾ tsp bicarbonate of soda [baking soda]
1 tsp mixed spice [pudding spice]
pinch of salt
1 large egg, lightly beaten

50ml/1¾fl oz milk
3 knobs of stem [preserved] ginger
  in syrup, roughly chopped
80g/2¾oz dark chocolate (between
  70–80% cocoa solids), roughly chopped

FOR THE FROSTING

80g/2¾oz unsalted butter, softened
  at room temperature
200g/7oz icing [confectioners'] sugar
1–2 Tbsp milk
2 tonka beans, finely grated,
  ideally on a microplane
pinch of salt

Preheat the oven to 180°C/350°F/Gas mark 4. Butter and line the base of a 20 × 20-cm/8 × 8-in brownie or baking tray with baking paper.

Place the butter, golden syrup, treacle, sugar, stem ginger syrup and fresh ginger in a pan over a medium heat. Let the mixture bubble away gently, stirring, until the sugar dissolves and everything is amalgamated. Remove the pan from the heat and leave to cool a little.

Meanwhile, using a fork or balloon whisk, whisk the flour, cocoa powder, bicarbonate of soda, mixed spice and salt together in a mixing bowl.

Whisk the egg into the melted butter and syrup mixture, then pour this liquid into the flour mixture. Stir well to combine, then gradually add the milk to make a slightly thin but not runny batter. Fold in the stem ginger pieces and chocolate. Pour into the prepared tray and bake for 30–35 minutes until firm on top. Leave in the tray for 10 minutes, then turn out onto a wire rack, carefully peel off the paper and leave to cool completely.

Meanwhile, make the frosting. Beat the butter in a stand mixer or in a bowl with electric beaters until pale and creamy. Beat in the icing sugar in 3 or 4 additions, scraping down the sides of the bowl now and then, and add enough of the milk to make a spreadable texture. Stir in the grated tonka bean and the salt.

Slather the top of the cooled cake with the frosting and cut into squares.

SALVADOR DALÍ-INSPIRED FLOURLESS
CHESTNUT, CHOCOLATE AND RUM CAKE

This gorgeously gooey flourless cake was inspired by 'Chocolate with Rum', a recipe in Salvador Dalí's fantastical cookbook *Les Diners de Gala*. It's one of my favourites. At once a cookbook and an art book, it combines Dalí's wild artistic imaginings with his passion for gastronomy. He and his wife Gala were famous for their lavish dinner parties: guests attended in costume, live monkeys decorated the room and meals were served in objects, including satin slippers. But food—including chocolate—was an inspiration for his Surrealist images as well as being one of life's great pleasures. His 1930 painting *Chocolate* depicts a woman in the shape of an urn, with chocolate dribbling from her mouth into a cup and onto an apple below. Dalí also famously appeared in a bizarre television advertisement for Lanvin chocolate, complete with an animated moustache.

There's nothing surreal about this very rich cake, which makes an excellent and easy dessert.

SERVES 8-10

300ml/10fl oz dark rum
150g/5¼oz pitted prunes
200g/7oz unsalted butter, roughly chopped, plus extra for greasing
200g/7oz dark chocolate (70% cocoa solids), chopped
200g/7oz caster [superfine] sugar
200g/7oz chestnut purée
3 large eggs, separated
generous pinch of salt
cocoa powder, for dusting (optional)
cold crème fraîche, to serve

Place the rum and prunes in a pan, bring to the boil, then reduce the heat and simmer gently for 10 minutes. Remove from the heat and leave to cool for at least 15 minutes.

Preheat the oven to 160°C/325°F/Gas mark 3 and butter and line the base of a 20-cm/8-in loose-bottomed or springform cake tin with baking paper.

Melt the chocolate in a heatproof bowl set over a pan of barely simmering water, making sure the bottom of the bowl doesn't touch the water. Remove the bowl from the pan and set aside to cool a little.

Place the butter, sugar, chestnut purée, egg yolks, salt and the prunes with their rum in a food processor and blitz until smooth and creamy. Add the melted, cooled chocolate and blitz again until completely combined. Scrape into a mixing bowl.

Beat the egg whites in a scrupulously clean bowl with electric beaters or in a stand mixer until stiff but not too firm or dry, or you won't be able to fold them easily into the chocolate mixture. Beat one-third of the egg whites into the chocolate mixture to loosen, then gently and gradually fold in the rest—don't be tempted to beat or you will lose the air. Spoon the batter into the prepared cake tin and smooth the top.

Bake for 1 hour–1 hour 15 minutes: when done, the cake should be dry and firm on top (but not springy, as it will be mousse-like in the centre) and coming away from the edges of the tin. Leave to cool in the tin for 10 minutes; it will shrink a bit but that is as it should be and will firm up a little as it cools. Release from the tin and sit on a wire rack to cool completely.

Dust with sifted cocoa—this isn't essential but adds a lovely bitter note—and serve with cold crème fraîche.

CHOCOLATE, FIG AND RYE CAKE WITH PX SHERRY AND CITRUS

Fragrant, rich and juicy with dried figs, this resembles a Christmas cake—but is much more delicious and interesting in my humble opinion. Dried fruit and molasses are key landmarks on the chocolate flavour map, so the ingredients make a fine match all round, especially the raisin-rich Pedro Ximénez sherry. Chocolate from the Dominican Republic or Grenada—redolent with raisins, spices, molasses and cocoa—works particularly well in this cake.

SERVES 8–10

300g/10½oz soft dried figs, chopped
150ml/5fl oz Pedro Ximénez sherry
120g/4¼oz unsalted butter, plus extra
  for greasing
150g/5¼oz honey
150g/5¼oz treacle [molasses]
2 large eggs, lightly beaten
125g/4½oz rye flour
125g/4½oz plain [all-purpose] flour
20g/¾oz cocoa powder

2 tsp baking powder
2 tsp ground cinnamon
½ star anise, ground
1½ tsp ground cardamom
¼ tsp ground nutmeg
generous pinch of salt
100ml/3½fl oz milk
100g/3½oz mixed candied citrus peel
150g/5¼oz dark chocolate (70% cocoa
  solids), chopped small

Place the figs in a small bowl, pour over the sherry and push the figs under to immerse. Set aside for a good 2 hours.

Preheat the oven to 180°C/350°F/Gas mark 4. Butter a 20-cm/8-in round cake tin and line the base with baking paper.

Melt the butter, honey and treacle together in a small pan over a medium heat. Simmer gently for 2 minutes, stirring frequently, then remove from the heat and leave to cool a little. Stir in the eggs.

Using a fork or balloon whisk, whisk the flours, cocoa, baking powder, spices and salt together in a bowl. Stir the butter mixture and the milk into the dry ingredients, then fold in the figs (and any sherry left in the bottom of the bowl), the mixed citrus peel and chocolate.

Scrape the batter into the prepared tin and bake for 50–60 minutes until firm on top and a skewer inserted into the centre comes out clean. Leave in the tin for 5 minutes, then run a knife around the edge of the cake and release from the tin. Leave to cool on a wire rack before cutting.

APRICOT AND BROWN BUTTER CRUMBLE
CAKE WITH CHOCOLATE AND RYE

The tangy floral sweetness of apricots brings a delicious fruitiness to dark chocolate as showcased in the famous Austrian chocolate cake, Sachertorte. Fun fact: during a protracted legal battle in the 1950s and 1960s between Vienna's Hotel Sacher and Demel's patisserie over who owned the original recipe for Sachertorte, apricot jam—and the placement thereof—was the nub of the legal wrangling. While Demel's spreads the jam only under the glossy chocolate icing, Hotel Sacher fills the middle of the cake with it as well. In the end, Hotel Sacher won the right to name its cake the original, but both still serve the confection in their own unique way. There's nothing contentious about this cake—it's unequivocally flavourful and lovely.

SERVES 8-10

125g/4½oz unsalted butter, plus extra for greasing

150g/5¼oz plain [all-purpose] flour

120g/4¼oz dark chocolate (80% cocoa solids), roughly chopped

1 tsp baking powder

½ tsp bicarbonate of soda [baking soda]

¼ tsp fine sea salt

160g/5¾oz caster [superfine] sugar

1 large egg

150ml/5fl oz sour cream

300–400g/10½–14oz whole fresh apricots, halved (and quartered if large) and stoned [pitted]

softly whipped cream, to serve (optional)

FOR THE CRUMBLE

100g/3½oz unsalted butter, melted

60g/2¼oz soft light brown sugar

40g/1½oz caster [superfine] sugar

1 tsp ground cinnamon

¼ tsp fine sea salt

130g/4½oz plain [all-purpose] flour

25g/1oz ground almonds

30g/1oz breadcrumbs made from a dark rye loaf

A couple of hours before you want to make the cake, prepare the brown butter. Place the 125g/4½oz unsalted butter in a light-coloured pan and cook over a medium heat, stirring frequently, until it turns dark brown and smells gloriously nutty. Pour into a heatproof bowl and set aside to solidify. (Once it's cooled a little you can transfer it to the fridge to expedite matters.)

When you're ready to make the cake, preheat the oven to 180°C/350°F/Gas mark 4. Lightly butter a 20-cm/8-in round loose-bottomed or springform cake tin and line the base with baking paper.

Start by making the crumble. Melt the 100g/3½oz butter and set aside. Place the remaining crumble ingredients in a bowl and, using a fork or balloon whisk, whisk to combine, then add the melted butter. Stir with a fork so the butter is completely combined and you have a mixture of large and small clumps. Chill while you make the cake.

For the cake, using a fork or balloon whisk, whisk the flour, chocolate, baking powder, bicarbonate of soda and salt together in a bowl.

Transfer the solidified brown butter to a mixing bowl or a stand mixer, add the sugar and beat together until pale and fluffy—the butter might be a little granular at first but keep beating and it will turn creamy. Beat in the egg, then the sour cream.

Add the flour mixture in several additions, beating after each one until just incorporated. You don't want to overbeat. Spoon the batter into the prepared tin and smooth the top.

Arrange enough apricot halves (or quarters) on top to cover completely— it doesn't matter which side up, as you won't see them—and push them into the batter a little. Scatter the crumble mixture evenly over the top making sure it's completely covered. (You might have to break up very large clumps.)

Bake for 1 hour 15 minutes until golden on top and cooked through. Leave in the tin for 10 minutes, then run a knife around the edge and release the cake. It's lovely served warm with a spoonful of softly whipped cream.

CHOCOLATE AND LIQUORICE LOAF CAKE WITH TREACLE SYRUP

This cake is inspired by Nigella Lawson's outrageously good quadruple chocolate loaf cake—a damp, squidgy creation that I've made many times. I've filled the cake with liquorice flavours that chime beautifully with the molasses notes in dark chocolate and adopted Nigella's idea to drench the top with syrup. The treacle adds a gorgeously rich, burnt caramel flavour, which in my mind inhabits the same heady realm as liquorice.

SERVES 8–10

115g/4oz unsalted butter, at room temperature, plus extra for greasing
270g/8½oz plain [all-purpose] flour
2 tsp baking powder
3 tsp liquorice powder
¼ tsp salt
70g/2½oz dark chocolate (70% cocoa solids), roughly chopped
100g/3½oz caster [superfine] sugar
70g/2½oz soft dark brown sugar

3 Tbsp treacle [molasses]
1 large egg, lightly beaten
200ml/6¾fl oz milk
80g/2¾oz dark chocolate chips

FOR THE SYRUP

125ml/4¼fl oz water
100g/3½oz caster [superfine] sugar
2 tsp cocoa powder
2 tsp treacle [molasses]

Preheat the oven to 160°C/325°F/Gas mark 3 and butter and line a standard 900-g/2-lb loaf tin.

Using a fork or balloon whisk, whisk the flour, baking powder, liquorice powder and salt together in a bowl and set aside.

Melt the chocolate in a heatproof bowl set over a pan of barely simmering water, making sure the bottom of the bowl doesn't touch the water. Remove the bowl from the pan and set aside.

Beat the butter, both the sugars and treacle together in a stand mixer or in a bowl with electric beaters until well combined and creamy. Beat in the melted chocolate and then the egg. Stir in the flour mixture, alternating with the milk, until just combined. Fold in the chocolate chips. Scrape the batter into the prepared loaf tin and bake for 50 minutes–1 hour until firm to the touch and coming away from the sides of the tin slightly.

To make the syrup, place all the ingredients in a small pan and simmer until slightly thickened. As soon as the cake comes out of the oven, poke holes all over the top of the hot cake with a skewer and pour over the syrup while still warm. Leave to cool completely in the tin before turning out.

APPLE AND CHOCOLATE CHIP RYE SHARING SCONE

Impress your food nerd friends with this fruity fact: Terry's famous Chocolate Orange (to which I am excessively partial) began life as an apple. Launched in 1926 by Terry's, the once York-based luxury chocolate maker, the 'Dessert Chocolate Apple' was shaped like its namesake and came segmented for easy sharing. Sophie Jewett, chocolate maker and founder of York Cocoa House, revealed to me (somewhat disappointingly, to be honest) that it wasn't apple flavoured. The design was simply a clever marketing wheeze aimed at wealthy chocolate lovers—the only people who could afford to buy it. "It was just a really beautiful and delicate way of sharing high-quality chocolate at the end of a meal," she explains. The chocolate apple proved so popular that Terry's returned to the fruit bowl for inspiration in 1932, when it launched the more exotic Chocolate Orange. Unsurprisingly, the orange-shaped confection—which was flavoured accordingly this time—proved a huge hit. Orange zest and orange-flower water had been popular chocolate flavourings since the seventeenth century, and oranges were still regarded as exotic fruits that symbolized wealth. By 1954 chocolate apple's time was up: when post-war rationing in the UK ended, it was never revived.

I'm very pleased to say that apple and chocolate are flavours that actually work very well together. You could serve slices of this oversized scone with a splodge of softly whipped cream on the side, as you would an individual version. But if you devour some fresh from the oven you need nothing more than an appetite.

SERVES 8

100g/3½oz cold unsalted butter, diced, plus extra for greasing

300g/10½oz plain [all-purpose] flour, plus extra for dusting

75g/2¾oz rye flour

50g/1¾oz caster [superfine] sugar, plus 2 Tbsp

1½ Tbsp baking powder

¼ tsp fine sea salt

100g/3½oz dark chocolate chips

1 large egg, lightly beaten

125ml/4¼fl oz whole milk

80g/2¾oz crème fraîche

2 medium eating apples

1 tsp ground cinnamon

Preheat the oven to 220°C/425°F/Gas mark 7 and butter a 20-cm/8-in round springform or loose-bottomed cake tin.

Sift both flours into a mixing bowl, adding the rye bran caught in the sieve back into the bowl. Add the 50g/1¾oz sugar, the baking powder and salt and whisk with a fork to combine. Rub the butter in with your fingertips until the mixture resembles coarse breadcrumbs. Fold in the chocolate chips.

Transfer 1 tablespoon each of the egg and milk to a small bowl or cup and mix well. Set aside.

Mix the remaining egg, crème fraîche and half the remaining milk together in a small jug or bowl, then stir this into the flour and chocolate mixture. Gradually add enough of the remaining milk to make a shaggy mass, stirring just enough to bring everything together.

Turn out onto a well-floured work surface and, using light hands — by which I mean don't press or squeeze, just touch lightly — briefly knead once or twice, then divide in half.

Lightly roll out one half into a 20-cm/8-in circle. You will need to sprinkle the work surface and rolling pin with flour to prevent sticking. Tuck this disc into the prepared tin.

Peel, core and finely slice the apples, then toss with the 2 tablespoons sugar and the cinnamon. Scatter the apple slices over the dough in the tin. Roll out the remaining piece of dough into another 20-cm/8-in circle and place on top of the apple. Tuck the edges into the sides of the tin.

Brush with the reserved egg and milk mixture and bake for about 25 minutes, or until the top is golden. It's best served warm and eaten on the day it's made.

EARL GREY TEA LOAF WITH CHOCOLATE CHUNKS

Cakes infused with tea can sometimes be a bit lacklustre in flavour, by which I mean they don't actually taste much of tea. Not here. The tea leaves are chopped finely and incorporated into the cake, so you can really appreciate the fragrant bergamot notes that work so beautifully with chocolate.

SERVES 8–10

180g/6oz unsalted butter, at room temperature, plus extra for greasing

8g/¼oz Earl Grey tea leaves (loose leaves are best but open up some tea bags if that's what you have)

180g/6oz plain [all-purpose] flour

100g/3½oz dark chocolate (ideally between 50–60% cocoa solids), roughly chopped

2 tsp baking powder

generous pinch of fine sea salt

150g/5¼oz soft light brown sugar

3 large eggs, lightly beaten

100g/3½oz Greek or natural yogurt

1 tsp vanilla extract

2–3 Tbsp milk

Preheat the oven to 180°C/350°F/Gas mark 4. Butter a standard 900-g/2-lb loaf tin and line the base with baking paper. If you're using loose leaf tea, blitz the leaves to a powder in a spice or coffee grinder.

Using a fork or balloon whisk, whisk the flour, tea, chocolate, baking powder and salt together in a bowl.

Beat the butter and sugar together in a stand mixer or in a bowl with electric beaters until very pale and fluffy—this will take a good 5 minutes.

Gradually beat in the eggs, adding 1 tablespoon of the flour mixture after the first addition to prevent the mixture from curdling. Beat for a few more minutes until well combined and fluffy, then beat in the yogurt and vanilla.

Add the remaining flour mixture and stir until just combined, then add enough of the milk to produce a batter that drops off the spoon easily.

Pour into the prepared tin and smooth the top. Bake for 40–45 minutes until firm on top and a skewer inserted in the centre comes out clean. Leave in the tin for 5 minutes then turn out onto a wire rack to cool.

This is delicious eaten warm while the chocolate is still a bit soft. Or enjoy any time in thick slices spread with cold salted butter.

BLACK SESAME SEED AND DARK CHOCOLATE BRIOCHE LOAF

This loaf is similar to Eastern European *babka*, a plaited loaf filled with chocolate that the world had gone crazy for as I was writing this book. My version uses black sesame seeds in the filling: I love their intense charcoal colour and the way they work brilliantly with chocolate. Unlike their white counterparts, black sesame seeds are still wearing their hulls, which impart a more intensely sesame, slightly bitter and smoky flavour. This makes a wickedly good treat for brunch: I exhort you to serve it warm.

SERVES 8

FOR THE BRIOCHE

250g/8¾oz strong white bread flour, plus extra for dusting

30g/1oz caster [superfine] sugar

7g/¼oz fast-action dried [active dry] yeast

½ tsp fine sea salt

3 large eggs, lightly beaten

150g/5¼oz unsalted butter, at room temperature, plus extra for greasing

flavourless vegetable oil, for oiling

1 egg, lightly beaten with a splash of milk, for egg wash

FOR THE FILLING

80g/2¾oz dark chocolate (70% cocoa solids), chopped

50g/1¾oz unsalted butter

2 tsp golden [corn] syrup or honey

50g/1¾oz black sesame seeds

40g/1½oz caster [superfine] sugar

15g/½oz cocoa powder

generous pinch of ground cinnamon

To make the brioche, place the flour, sugar, yeast and salt in a stand mixer and stir to combine. Add the eggs. Using the dough hook attachment, mix on low speed for 5 minutes, stopping to scrape down the bowl a couple of times until all the flour is incorporated. Increase the speed to medium and mix for 10 minutes until it looks like a sticky dough.

Reduce the speed to low and add small pieces of the butter, a few at a time — adding more once they're amalgamated. When all the butter is used up, increase the speed to medium and mix for a further 10 minutes until the dough is shiny and elastic and comes away from the sides of the bowl cleanly,

Lightly butter a large mixing bowl. Tip the dough onto a work surface and press out to form a rectangle about 2.5cm/1in thick. Working left to right, fold one-third of the dough over itself, then do the same with the right side. Repeat with the top and the bottom. Place the dough, seam-side down, in the prepared bowl, cover with plastic wrap and set aside somewhere warm for an hour.

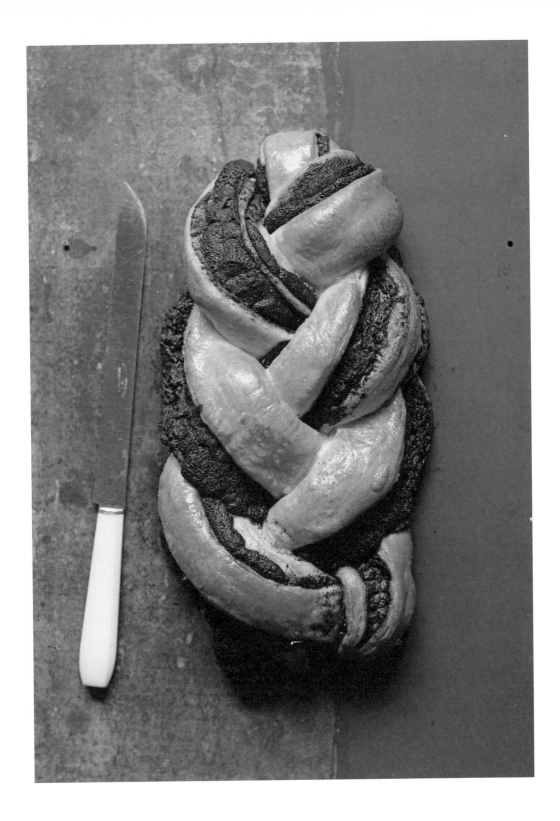

Tip the dough out onto a work surface, gently press into a rectangle and fold as before. Chill for at least 1 hour — it has to be well chilled and firm to work with.

Now, make the filling. Place the chocolate, butter and golden syrup or honey in a heatproof bowl set over a pan of barely simmering water, making sure the bottom of the bowl doesn't touch the water, stirring now and then, until melted.

Blitz the sesame seeds in a spice or coffee grinder — they turn to a paste fairly quickly, but that's fine. Add to the chocolate mixture, along with the remaining filling ingredients and beat with a wooden spoon until very well combined. Set aside at room temperature to cool completely and firm up a little. Meanwhile, line a baking sheet with baking paper and dust with flour. Set aside.

Once the dough has chilled, roll into a square roughly 30 × 30cm / 11¾ × 11¾in. Spread with the chocolate filling, leaving a 1-cm / ⅜-in border all around. Pull the edge closest to you up and over the filling and roll into a log. Carefully transfer to the prepared baking sheet and return to the fridge to firm up for 1 hour.

Using a rolling pin, gently flatten the log into a long rectangle about 30cm / 11¾in long and 12cm / 4¾in wide. Use a sharp knife, cut lengthways into 3 × 4-cm / 1½-in strips, leaving 2cm / ¾in at the top uncut so they stay together. Plait the strips, then press the ends together and tuck underneath. Cover loosely with oiled plastic wrap and set aside to rise for 1 hour.

Meanwhile, preheat the oven to 150°C / 300°F / Gas mark 2. Brush the loaf with the egg wash and bake for 40 minutes until risen and golden. Serve warm, in thick slices.

HONEYED WHEATEN BREAD WITH OATMEAL AND NIBS

The nibs deliver little bursts of mildly bitter cocoa flavour in this simple, delicious loaf. It's not overly sweet—the honey just hovers pleasingly in the background —so it's lovely served in thick slices with soup, as an accompaniment to cheese, or just spread with cold salted butter. Also, it's a doddle to make.

SERVES 8-10

60g/2¼oz cold butter, cut into small cubes, plus extra for greasing

180g/6oz wholemeal [wholewheat] flour

180g/6oz plain [all-purpose] flour

30g/1oz porridge oats, plus extra for scattering on top

pinch of salt

1 tsp bicarbonate of soda [baking soda]

30g/1oz cacao nibs

3 Tbsp honey

300ml/10fl oz buttermilk

2 Tbsp milk, if needed

Preheat the oven to 180°C/350°F/Gas mark 4 and butter a standard 900-g/2-lb loaf tin.

Using a fork or balloon whisk, whisk the flours, oats, salt and bicarbonate of soda together in a bowl. Rub in the butter with your fingertips until the mixture resembles breadcrumbs.

Pulse the nibs briefly in a food processor—you want to chop up any large pieces. Add to the flour and butter mixture and stir to evenly distribute.

Stir the honey into the buttermilk, then pour into the dry mixture and stir to make a shaggy, sticky dough. Add the milk if it seems too dry.

Spoon the batter into the prepared tin, making sure it's spread evenly and fills the corners. Smooth the top. Scatter over a small handful of oats and gently press them down so they stick.

Bake for 40 minutes, or until risen and golden, and a skewer inserted into the centre comes out clean. Leave in the tin for 10 minutes, then turn out on a wire rack to cool.

CHOCOLATE, CHILLI AND LIME CORNBREAD

The idea for this cake came to me as I devoured a chocolate *tamale* at Mucho, a remarkable chocolate shop, café and museum in Mexico City. *Tamales* are an ancient food made with corn-based dough, commonly filled with meat, cheese or vegetables, and wrapped in a corn husk for cooking. But, as I discovered, chocolate also works very well in a *tamale*, as it pairs beautifully with the mild, earthy sweetness of corn. I originally intended this as a sweet cake, but my husband suggested you could also serve it the same way you would conventional cornbread, that is, alongside a spicy chilli or the Pork Carnitas on page 200. Reader, he was correct.

SERVES 8

FOR THE CORNBREAD

2 Tbsp olive oil, plus extra for oiling
180ml/6fl oz natural [plain] yogurt
2 large eggs
60ml/2fl oz lime juice
finely grated zest of 2 limes
200g/7oz cornmeal
70g/2½oz masa flour or plain
  [all-purpose] flour

40g/1½oz cocoa powder
1 tsp bicarbonate of soda [baking soda]
75g/2¾oz soft light brown sugar
2 tsp crushed chipotle chillies

FOR THE LIME AND MAPLE BUTTER

100g/3½oz unsalted butter, softened
2–3 Tbsp maple syrup
finely grated zest of 3 limes

Generously brush a 20-cm/8-in round baking dish with oil and place in a 200°C/400°F/Gas mark 6 oven to heat up.

Beat the yogurt, eggs, the 2 tablespoons of oil, the lime juice and zest together in a bowl.

In a separate bowl, whisk the remaining cornbread ingredients together, then stir the wet ingredients into the dry. Quickly pour into the hot baking dish, smooth the top and bake for about 30 minutes.

While the cornbread is cooking, beat all the lime and maple butter ingredients together in a bowl—electric beaters work best here.

Serve the cornbread hot from the oven with the butter on top.

"Chocolate rivers flowed on a number of swiftly moving conveyors through gaps in the wall to mysterious chambers beyond. Solid chocolate shaped in a myriad of exciting confections travelled in neat, soldierly processions towards the wrapping department. Such a miracle of clockwork precision and sensual extravagance was hard to take in." —Deborah Cadbury, *Chocolate Wars*

Melting a piece of chocolate in your mouth is perhaps the most sensual food experience. The sweet, complex aroma as it passes under the nose, the buttery smoothness on the tongue, the sublime confluence of sugar, fat and cocoa, and the burst of flavour as it dissolves all combine to make chocolate truly beguiling. But it didn't always have this pull on our senses.

For most of its history, chocolate was a rather bitter, fatty and not entirely pleasant drink. Our love affair only really began with industrialization and the first chocolate bar for eating, invented in 1847 by Joseph Fry, founder of the British firm J.S. Fry & Sons. Fry squeezed the cocoa butter from cocoa mass (the paste made from ground up roasted cacao beans) using Coenraad van Houten's press (page 73) and then ingeniously added some of it back in to produce a rich liquid chocolate that could be poured into moulds and set to make solid bars.

Other British brands, including Cadbury, Rowntree's and Terry's of York, and chocolate factories in Europe and the US quickly tried to emulate the process. The bars they produced weren't perfect—still dry, gritty and dark—but chocolate pioneers in Switzerland soon set about tackling these problems. François-Louis Cailler, Philippe Suchard and others developed techniques that vastly improved the way cacao beans were ground and refined, resulting in smoother but still grainy chocolate.

This problem was finally resolved in 1879 when Rodolphe Lindt invented the 'conche', a machine that continuously stirred and aerated cocoa mass using heavy granite rollers. Various conching methods are used to make chocolate today, but in Lindt's time, the process probably made chocolate smoother, developed its flavour and reduced bitterness. Around the same time, Daniel Peter and Henri Nestlé—pause for a moment's silence in their honour—produced the first milk chocolate. After years of experimenting, Peter hit upon the idea to use milk powder made from condensed milk, invented by his friend and neighbour Nestlé. It was an entirely new kind of confectionery, and it took the world by storm.

By the end of the nineteenth century, chocolate was being manufactured on an industrial scale and transported far and wide by rail. It was also cheaper than ever before; in the 1890s and 1900s cacao prices fell, as supplies increased following the expansion of cacao plantations to Africa and beyond. The fall in price reduced returns for cacao growers but facilitated chocolate's transition from exclusive privilege of the rich to affordable snacks for the masses.

As consumers' taste for chocolate grew, manufacturers competed aggressively for their business, and rivalry between British firms, and with the Swiss, was intense. Chocolate makers needed to innovate constantly and sharpen their marketing strategies to survive. Although they no longer touted chocolate as a medicine, manufacturers promoted milk chocolate as a form of healthy nourishment. Advertising posters featured happy rosy-cheeked children, Alpine scenes with cows roaming through verdant fields and nurturing mothers feeding their families, creating a wholesome halo around chocolate bars. In 1928 Cadbury launched its 'glass and a half' campaign to explain the amount of milk in every bar, appealing to consumers' faith in the white stuff as a pure and healthy food staple. It was a huge success and the 'glass and a half' symbol is still the face of the company.

Manufacturers were also quick to realize chocolate's potential as something more than just food. Richard Cadbury, who ran the company with his brother George after taking over from their father in 1861, is credited with creating the first 'chocolate box' in 1868. Adorned with a painting of his young daughter Jessica holding a kitten, it began a fashion for beautiful chocolate boxes bedecked with romantic and sentimental illustrations. The boxes were more than packaging; they were intended for keeping, perhaps to store mementos, forging the first links between chocolate and nostalgia.

In 1912, the chocolate box became even more appealing when Belgian chocolatier Jean Neuhaus II devised a way to enrobe a soft filling or 'praline' with a hard shell of chocolate. The mixed boxed assortment became a fixture in the chocolate firmament when Cadbury launched its Milk Tray in 1915 — a no-frills selection designed for 'everyday eating'.

Manufacturers quickly realized that chocolate could bring joy in many forms. In the early nineteenth century, confectioners in France and Germany produced Europe's first chocolate Easter eggs. They were probably inspired by the famous Fabergé egg, the jewelled creation crafted by the House of Fabergé for the Russian royal family that triggered a global fashion for elaborately decorated ovoids. Fry's was the first to launch Easter eggs in the UK in 1873, followed two years later by Cadbury with a dark chocolate range filled with sugared almonds.

After the huge success of its Dairy Milk chocolate in 1905, Cadbury started production of milk chocolate eggs, and then eggs filled with cream. The Creme Egg in its current iconic form was introduced in 1963; the white and yellow fondant-filled treats are now manufactured all over the world. The Bourneville factory in Birmingham alone is said to churn out 1.5 million each day.

Chocolate love wasn't confined to the UK and Europe, of course. Dr James Baker set up the first US chocolate factory in 1765 with the help of Irish immigrant John Hannan. The firm remained a family business for generations, and became known for its *La Belle Chocolatière* logo, a painting by Swiss artist Jean-Étienne Liotard of a beautiful girl bearing a tray of hot chocolate. (Although Baker's Chocolate is now owned by the Kraft Heinz Company, a version of the painting still figures on its packaging). A few years later chocolatier Étienne Guittard set sail from France bound for San Francisco, where he became the leading supplier of quality chocolate for confectioners, bakers and ice cream makers.

Once machinery was available to do the job, chocolate production and distribution were ready for a seismic shift, and US confectionery entrepreneur and industrialist Milton Hershey, seized the opportunity. He launched the Hershey Bar in 1894 and set out to make it affordable for everyone by manufacturing it in vast quantities, cheaply. By 1906 he had not just built a factory but a whole chocolate town — Hershey, Pennsylvania. With houses, transport systems, churches, shops and even a zoo for workers and their children, it was a more elaborate version of the model factories in England run by Cadbury, Fry's and Rowntree's that supplied housing and education for employees. (The town of Hershey, an associated theme park and other amusements continue to prosper.)

Although the distinctively sour, cheesy taste of Hershey's has never been fully embraced worldwide, US chocolate lovers have developed an unstinting taste for it. (The flavour is thought to stem from the breakdown of milk fat, which develops a slight note of rancidity.) Hershey's kisses, the teardrop-shaped morsels, were launched in 1907 and are still one of the most popular chocolates in the US. By 1911, Hershey's turnover had soared to $US5 million, dwarfing sales of his European counterparts. Just over a decade later, Frank Mars, founder of the Mars corporation, developed the Milky Way bar (known outside the US as Mars bars), which was an instant sensation. Cheaper than solid chocolate bars because it contained less actual chocolate—just a coating over layers of nougat and caramel—it paved the way for an explosion of chocolate confectionery products. The world's appetite for chocolate was unstoppable.

WHY DO WE LIKE CHOCOLATE?

In 2017, more than 7 million tonnes of chocolate confectionery were consumed globally, according to Euro Monitor, and chocolate is now the most craved food in the Western world. So, what is it about chocolate that makes us desire it so? Scientists have been trying to fathom the reasons for decades.

One possibility is that we're hardwired to like milk chocolate because its sugar-to-fat ratio is similar to that of breast milk (around 1g fat to 2g sugars). It's also suggested that some of the hundreds of chemical compounds in chocolate are psychoactive and can affect the pleasure centres of the brain. These include the so-called 'bliss molecule' anandamide, which works in a similar way to cannabis; tyramine and phenylethylamine, thought to have similar affects to amphetamines; tryptophan and serotonin, which influence mood and behaviour; and the stimulants caffeine and theobromine.

Some studies suggest that some of these compounds can trigger a surge of dopamine, a neurotransmitter that helps control the brain's reward and pleasure centres. However, scientists generally agree that there probably aren't enough of these compounds in chocolate to have a significant effect (unless you actually binge on vast quantities). In fact, a fascinating study by the University of Pennsylvania in the 1990s suggests there is much more to chocolate's appeal than its chemical components. Chocolate cravers were given milk chocolate, white chocolate and a pill containing the minerals and pharmacologically active ingredients of cacao. They reported that consuming the compounds in pill form did not satisfy their desire for chocolate.

A more likely explanation for chocolate's appeal is just beginning to emerge from the work of scientists researching addiction. Evidence suggests that the combination of sugar and fat in chocolate can trigger symptoms similar to drug addiction.

New imaging techniques are beginning to shed light on what actually happens in our brains when we feel an overwhelming desire for certain foods. "Highly processed foods like chocolate may be capable of engaging addiction-like neural circuitry in a similar manner as drugs of abuse," explains Dr Erica Schulte, from the Food Addiction Science and Treatment Lab at the University of Michigan. "Individuals with obesity respond similarly to highly processed foods as people with substance-use disorders do to their drug of abuse."

But what about the gorgeously luscious texture of chocolate and the way it melts in the mouth? These features also make chocolate hugely appealing. Cacao beans contain roughly 55% cocoa butter, which has at least six different crystal forms, each with its own melting point. The science is complex, but Form V is the one favoured by consumers and the chocolate industry; with a melting point of 33–34°C [91–93°F], just below human body temperature, it slowly melts when placed on the tongue. Special receptors send signals to the brain, which finds this textural change highly pleasurable, explains Dr Barry Smith, director of the Centre for the Study of the Senses at Birkbeck University of London. "When you have something that passes slowly and deliciously across the mouth with the kind of viscosity and smoothness of chocolate, you're getting the same sort of seductive pleasure, the hedonics, as being gently stroked," he says. If it sounds like eating chocolate is an almost erotic experience, consider this: a small study in 2007 found that melting chocolate in the mouth was more pleasurable than passionate kissing.

But chocolate's aroma is also important. Dr Smith explains that the brain processes aromas slightly differently when we sniff them (orthonasal olfaction) compared to when they travel to the back of the nose through the mouth (retronasal olfaction). This accounts for the fact that brewed coffee doesn't taste quite as wonderful as it smells, and some strong cheese tastes better than its stinky aroma suggests. "With chocolate, the pleasure of anticipation triggered by the smell and the reward in eating it matches up," Dr Smith says. "The brain really likes that because it's predicting something and then gets it as an extra reward. It's part of why chocolate is such a wonder food."

DOES SHAPE AFFECT TASTE?

Professor Charles Spence, an experimental psychologist at the University of Oxford, researches how our brains use all of our senses to perceive food. His work suggests clear and perhaps surprising connections between chocolate and our senses. Our experience of eating chocolate, he says, is affected by its shape: we associate sweetness with roundness, and bitterness with angularity. One fascinating possibility is that chocolate's flavour can actually be enhanced or diminished by altering its shape.

In 2013, Cadbury changed the design of the segments in its Dairy Milk bar from rectangular to curved. The change coincided with a public outcry that Cadbury had changed the recipe to make the bars sweeter, a claim the company denies. "It would appear that changing the shape of a confectionery item like Dairy Milk by rounding off the corners, without introducing any change whatsoever to the product formulation, can indeed alter the consumer's product experience," Professor Spence has theorized. He has also shown that 'sonic seasoning' can alter the taste of chocolate. Working with the Michelin-starred chocolatier Dominique Persoone in Belgium, he demonstrated that playing 'creamy' music (slow and legato) in his stores caused customers to find that his chocolates tasted extra creamy.

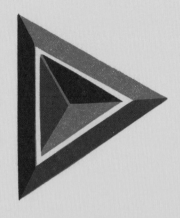

RICH AND GOOEY

BAKED CHOCOLATE SOUR CHERRY PUDDINGS
WITH KIRSCH AND BROWN SUGAR COFFEE CREAM

Black Forest Gateau—*Schwarzwälder Kirschtorte* in German—is a layered chocolate cake confection oozing whipped cream, sour cherries and booze, which stood proud on many British restaurants' dessert menus in the '70s. Dark, intense and crazily extravagant, it traditionally includes the sour Morello cherries that grow in the Black Forest region of Germany. This is my paean to *Schwarzwälder Kirschtorte*, but in pudding form: it's absurdly simple to make and outrageously good to eat. Regrettably, Morello cherries can be difficult to get hold of these days, although German speciality shops generally stock them. If you can find jars with kirsch already in the syrup, so much the better: you might not want to add the extra kirsch as instructed in my recipe, but I'm not going to tell you not to.

SERVES 4 GENEROUSLY

about 250g/8¾oz sour black cherries (drained weight) from a can or jar, ideally Morello (ordinary black cherries from a can or jar will do at a pinch), plus 150ml/5fl oz syrup reserved

50g/1¾oz unsalted butter

180g/6oz dark chocolate (between 70–80% cocoa solids), roughly chopped

3 large eggs

150g/5¼oz caster [superfine] sugar

¼ tsp fine sea salt

2 Tbsp cacao nibs (optional)

¼ tsp freshly ground black pepper

1–2 Tbsp kirsch, to taste

toasted flaked [slivered] almonds, to serve

FOR THE ESPRESSO CREAM

200ml/6¾fl oz double [heavy] cream

½ tsp espresso powder dissolved in ½ tsp boiling water

1 Tbsp soft dark brown sugar

Preheat the oven to 190°C/375°F/Gas mark 5.

Distribute the cherries between 4 × 400-ml/14-fl oz ovenproof bowls. Place on a rimmed baking sheet and set aside.

Melt the butter and chocolate together in a heatproof bowl set over a pan of barely simmering water, making sure the bottom of the bowl doesn't touch the water and stirring frequently until smooth. Remove the bowl from the pan and set aside to cool a little.

Meanwhile, whisk the eggs, 75g/2¾oz of the sugar and the salt together in a stand mixer or in a bowl with electric beaters until very pale, thick and significantly increased in volume—this will take a good 5 minutes. Fold in the melted chocolate in 3 batches, then the nibs (if using) and pepper.

Pour the chocolate mixture evenly over the cherries and bake for about 20 minutes —the puddings will have a lovely crust on top and be gooey in the middle.

While the puddings are cooking, place the reserved cherry syrup in a small pan with the remaining sugar and simmer for 2 minutes, or until the sugar has dissolved. Add the kirsch and simmer for 4 minutes until syrupy. Have a taste, adding more sugar or kirsch if you feel the need. Remove the pan from the heat and set aside.

Whip all the cream ingredients together in a stand mixer or in a bowl with electric beaters until the mixture barely holds its shape.

Serve the puddings hot from the oven: I like to make a little crater in the middle in which to place a spoonful or two of the cream. Drizzle with the cherry syrup, then scatter with toasted flaked almonds and serve immediately.

CHOCOLATE AND YUZU LAVA CAKES

Alongside fusion food and Cosmopolitans, chocolate fondants (or lava cakes) were the apogee of chic in the 1990s. The love child of a chocolate soufflé and a sponge cake, the dessert's origin is hotly contested. US chef Jean-Georges Vongerichten is widely claimed to have invented it in New York City in 1987, while French chef and chocolatier Jacques Torres says *pfft*! to that, such a dish already existed in France in the form of *le petit gateau*. Whatever, it eventually found its way into domestic kitchens, earning a certain reputation for being the pudding of choice for home cooks keen to flash their culinary skills. This is perplexing for me. Delicious as fondants are, I've only ever found cooking them very stressful: a blink of an eye stands between gooey success and dry sponge failure, and you only know which one it is once you have served them and guests have tucked in.

This version, filled with curd, is much more forgiving, and the citrus lends a fresh, bright note to what really is a very rich dessert. I've used yuzu, a citrus fruit popular in Japan, because I am obsessed with its lemon-lime-tangerine zing, and it's now widely available. But I've also made it with lime juice with lovely results.

The recipe makes more curd than you need, so store leftovers in the fridge for slathering on toast or swirling into Greek yogurt.

MAKES 6 CAKES (WITH CURD LEFT OVER)

FOR THE YUZU CURD
45ml/1½fl oz yuzu juice (lime juice also works nicely)
100g/3½oz caster [superfine] sugar
1 large egg
pinch of sea salt
25g/1oz cold unsalted butter, diced small

FOR THE CAKES
150g/5¼oz unsalted butter, softened, plus extra for greasing
60g/2¼oz cocoa powder, plus an extra 2–3 Tbsp, for dusting
90g/3¼oz plain [all-purpose] flour
pinch of salt
120g/4¼oz caster [superfine] sugar
3 large eggs, lightly beaten
3 Tbsp cold espresso coffee
vanilla ice cream or cream, to serve

First, make the curd. Place all the curd ingredients, except the butter, in a heatproof bowl set over a pan of barely simmering water. Stir constantly for 10 minutes until thick enough to cling to a wooden spoon: be careful not to overheat the mixture or it will curdle. Whisk in the butter, bit by bit. Carefully take the bowl off the pan and set aside to cool to room temperature, then transfer to the fridge.

Preheat the oven to 200°C/400°F/Gas mark 6. Butter 4 dariole moulds or ramekins with a 160ml/5½fl oz capacity, then dust with the 2–3 tablespoons cocoa powder, tipping out any excess cocoa, and place the moulds on a rimmed baking sheet.

Using a fork or balloon whisk, whisk the flour, cocoa powder and salt together in a bowl to combine. Set aside.

Beat the butter and sugar together in a stand mixer or in a bowl with electric beaters until pale and fluffy — this will take a good 5 minutes. Gradually beat in the eggs and then the espresso. Stir in the flour mixture until well incorporated. Fill each mould three-quarters full with the batter, then make a well in the centre and spoon in the curd. Cover completely with the remaining batter.

Bake for 17–18 minutes until risen and springy to touch. Run a knife around the edges of the moulds, then invert onto plates and serve immediately with vanilla ice cream or cream.

APPLE AND CHOCOLATE STRUDEL

This lush strudel-style dessert is based on the ancient Italian dish *rocciata*, a speciality in Umbria and the Marche traditionally prepared for All Saints Day, the Christian festival held in honour of all the saints, known and unknown. There are endless variations and each family has its own closely guarded recipe, but the classic version is a snake of pastry filled with apples, dried fruit soaked in alcohol, chocolate, nuts and spices. It's lovely to bring to the table whole, trailing the heady aromas behind you—with a helper bringing up the rear armed with a bowl of gently whipped cream for serving.

SERVES 8

FOR THE PASTRY

200g/7oz plain [all-purpose] flour, plus extra for dusting
40g/1½oz icing [confectioners'] sugar
pinch of fine sea salt
3 Tbsp olive oil
about 90ml/3fl oz white wine
softly whipped cream, to serve

FOR THE FILLING

60g/2¼oz soft dried figs
45g/1½oz sultanas [golden raisins]
4 Tbsp Vin Santo (Marsala, Oloroso sherry or any sweet wine will work well)

400g/14oz red eating apples, about 3 medium apples
few squeezes of lemon juice
finely grated zest of ½ lemon
40g/1½oz pine nuts
40g/1½oz walnuts, chopped
1 tsp ground cinnamon
1 Tbsp cocoa powder
4 Tbsp demerara [light brown] sugar, plus extra for sprinkling
40g/1½oz dark chocolate (between 70–80% cocoa solids), chopped small
1 egg, lightly beaten with a splash of milk, for egg wash

Start with the pastry. Using a fork or balloon whisk, whisk the flour, sugar and salt together in a bowl. Make a well in the centre, pour in the olive oil and then stir it into the flour. Gradually stir in enough of the wine to make a shaggy dough. Bring the mixture together with your hands and knead once or twice on a lightly floured work surface. Shape into a rectangle, wrap in plastic wrap and chill for 2 hours.

Meanwhile, for the filling, chop the figs into pieces about the size of your little fingernail and place in a small bowl with the sultanas. Pour over the Vin Santo, stir and set aside.

Preheat the oven to 180°C/350°F/Gas mark 4. Peel and core the apples and cut them into quarters. Cut each quarter in half lengthways and then finely slice crossways. Transfer to a mixing bowl and toss with a little lemon juice as you go to prevent browning. Add the lemon zest, nuts, cinnamon, cocoa, sugar, chocolate and the dried fruit and soaking liquor. Stir so all the ingredients are well distributed.

On a large sheet of floured baking paper (at least 55 × 30cm/22 × 12in), roll the chilled dough into a rectangle, roughly 50cm × 25cm/20 × 9¾in. With the long side parallel to the work surface, spread the filling evenly over the top, pressing down gently with the back of a spoon, leaving a 1–2cm/⅜–¾in border all around. Lightly brush the border with egg wash.

Fold the border of the dough closest to you over the fruit, then carefully roll into a long neat log: don't roll too tightly or the inner layers of dough won't cook properly, and be careful not to tear the dough, as the filling will leak out during cooking. Press the ends together to seal, then shape into a horseshoe or circle. Slide the paper onto a large baking sheet, brush all over with egg wash and sprinkle with demerara sugar. Bake for 45 minutes until golden and crisp underneath. The filling will be very hot, so leave to cool for at least 10 minutes before serving with clouds of whipped cream.

CHOCOLATE POTS WITH MEZCAL, THYME AND BLACKBERRIES

This is based on a sublime recipe by food writer Jane Grigson in her classic cookbook, *English Food*. Her version features white wine and rosemary, which I've replaced with tequila and thyme. You can increase the quantity of tequila if you fancy something boozier—just reduce the amount of water by the same amount. Glorious.

SERVES 4
80g/2¾oz dark chocolate (60% cocoa solids), grated or blitzed to a rubble in a food processor
60ml/2fl oz mezcal or tequila
60ml/2fl oz water
115g/4oz caster [superfine] sugar
1 Tbsp lemon juice

300ml/10fl oz double [heavy] cream
1 Tbsp thyme leaves, plus extra sprigs and/or flowers to serve

TO SERVE
1 handful of blackberries
crème fraîche

Have the chocolate ready by the hob [stove] in a heatproof bowl.

Place the mezcal, water, sugar and lemon juice in a small pan and stir. Set over a low heat and cook until the sugar dissolves: don't boil, as too much of the liquid will evaporate.

Add the cream and thyme and cook over a medium heat until the mixture is hot but not boiling. Slowly pour the cream over the chocolate, stirring constantly, until the chocolate has completely melted. Scrape the mixture back into the pan, return to a medium heat and simmer gently for 20 minutes, or until thick and glossy.

Distribute the chocolate mixture between 4 × small pots or espresso cups with a minimum 100ml/3½fl oz capacity. Cover with plastic wrap and set aside until cooled to room temperature, then chill for 1 hour, or until set.

Serve with blackberries on top, a splodge of crème fraîche and a sprig of thyme.

SALTED HONEY, PEAR AND CHOCOLATE TARTE TATIN

This is one of my very favourite desserts in this book, and not just because I'm a sucker for tarte Tatin. Salty caramel, roasted pear, crisp pastry and walnuts (sadly neglected since pistachios muscled into nut top spot) fuse into something completely delicious. I love the way the chocolate surreptitiously enriches the caramel, without shouting about it.

SERVES 4-6

1 sheet ready-rolled puff pastry or 320g/11¼oz block
plain [all-purpose] flour, for dusting (optional)
6 Conference pears (or other small pears), about 100g/3½oz each
lemon juice, for squeezing

70g/2½oz unsalted butter, chopped
70g/2½oz caster [superfine] sugar
70g/2½oz runny honey
½ tsp fine sea salt
50g/1¾oz walnut pieces
50g/1¾oz dark chocolate (60% cocoa solids), chopped
whipped cream, to serve

Preheat the oven to 180°C/350°F/Gas mark 4.

If using block pastry, roll out on a lightly floured work surface until 3mm/⅛in thick. Cut a 23-cm/9-in disc from the pastry, prick all over with a fork and chill.

Peel and halve the pears, then carefully remove the cores with a teaspoon: you want perfect halves if possible. Transfer to a bowl and toss with a little lemon juice as you go to prevent browning.

Melt the butter in a 20-cm/8-in ovenproof frying pan. Sprinkle over the sugar and cook for 2 minutes until it begins to dissolve, then stir in the honey and salt. Arrange all but one of the pears, cut-side up, in the pan with the narrowest end pointing to the centre—you want them to fit snugly as they will shrink slightly during cooking. If there is a space left right in the centre, cut a round from the remaining pear half and place it, cut-side up, in the space.

Cook over a medium heat for 30 minutes: the butter and sugar mixture should energetically bubble away and reduce down to a thick and syrupy amber-coloured caramel. Shake the pan frequently, and now and then spoon some caramel over the pears. Remove the pan from the heat and sprinkle over the walnuts and chocolate, filling in any gaps between the pears with the nuts. Cover with the pastry disc and tuck the edges into the sides of the pan with a spoon.

Bake for 30 minutes, or until puffed and golden. Set aside for 5 minutes, then carefully invert onto a plate. Serve immediately with whipped cream.

CHOCOLATE MOUSSE WITH SESAME HONEYCOMB AND OLIVE OIL

I was determined to devise my own version of this sublime dessert after scoffing platefuls of it at London restaurant Lupins. The combination of intense dark chocolate, sweet-salty-chewy honeycomb, sesame seeds and grassy olive oil is, as one reviewer described it, 'an outrageous creation'. She was correct. Add the very best chocolate and olive oil you can afford.

SERVES 4

FOR THE MOUSSE

150g/5¼oz dark chocolate (between
    70–75% cocoa solids), finely chopped
2 large egg yolks
20g/¾oz caster [superfine] sugar
75ml/2½fl oz whole milk
175ml/6fl oz double [heavy] cream

FOR THE HONEYCOMB

40g/1½oz white sesame seeds
1 tsp bicarbonate of soda [baking soda]
100g/3½oz caster [superfine] sugar
2 Tbsp golden [corn] syrup
1 Tbsp honey
good-quality extra virgin olive oil,
    rosemary-infused if you have it,
    for drizzling

Start with the mousse. Have the chocolate ready by the hob [stove] in a heatproof bowl. Whisk the egg yolks and sugar in a stand mixer or in a heatproof bowl with electric beaters until pale and creamy.

Combine the milk and cream in a pan and bring to a simmer. Pour the hot milk over the egg yolk mixture, whisking constantly. Return the mixture to the pan and cook over a medium heat, stirring constantly, for 5–10 minutes until it has thickened to a custard-like consistency: when you lift a wooden spoon out of it, it should stay coated. Pour the custard over the chopped chocolate and stir until melted and glossy, then pour through a sieve [strainer] into a bowl. Cover with plastic wrap, making sure it sticks to the chocolate to prevent a skin forming. Chill for 2 hours, or until set. Remove from the fridge 30 minutes before serving.

For the honeycomb, line a baking sheet with baking paper and have the sesame seeds and bicarbonate of soda measured out and ready by the hob. Place the sugar, golden syrup and honey in a high-sided pan and stir to combine. Set the pan over a medium heat and simmer until the mixture has turned a deep amber colour (a drop spooned into a glass of cold water should turn hard). Remove the pan from the heat and quickly stir in the sesame seeds and then the bicarbonate of soda. Stir constantly as the mixture froths up. Quickly pour onto the prepared baking sheet and leave for about 1 hour, or until hard. Break into pieces.

To serve, use 2 dessertspoons to scoop the mousse into oval shapes (quenelles) and place a couple of these in the centre of each serving plate. Sprinkle over some of the honeycomb pieces and drizzle with the olive oil. Serve immediately.

CHOCOLATE AND CHESTNUT APPLE CRUMBLE

I admit I was hesitant about tinkering with a national treasure. Believed to have been born during World War II butter rationing, fruit crumble figures large in the pantheon of adored British comfort foods. Over the years, though, it has evolved from a very modest arrangement of fruit topped with a mixture made from flour, sugar and fat, into a pudding with a great deal more to say. Spices, nuts, an assortment of grains and flours are now added as a matter of course — my mum always included oats and sultanas in hers. So, I don't think chocolate should rock the apple crumble cart too much. What's most important is that it's comforting and delicious.

SERVES 4-6
1kg/2¼lb eating apples
1 lemon, for squeezing
custard, cream or ice cream, to serve

FOR THE CRUMBLE
50g/1¾oz plain [all-purpose] flour
50g/1¾oz chestnut flour (or plain
  [all-purpose] flour)

50g/1¾oz ground almonds
pinch of salt
125g/4½oz cold butter, finely chopped
80g/2¾oz caster [superfine] sugar
50g/1¾oz cocoa powder
3 Tbsp cacao nibs
50g/1¾oz porridge oats

Preheat the oven to 200°C/400°F/Gas mark 6.

First, make the crumble. Using a fork or balloon whisk, whisk the flours, ground almonds and salt together in a bowl, then rub the butter in with your fingertips to make a rough breadcrumb consistency. Stir in the remaining crumble ingredients, so that everything is evenly distributed. Transfer to the freezer until needed (place the mixture in a plastic bag if it makes life easier).

Peel, core and quarter the apples, then cut into chunks, transferring them to a large pan as you go. Toss with a squeeze of lemon juice after each apple. Add a splash of water and cook, covered, for 5 minutes or so, shaking the pan often, until softened. Scoop out the apples with a slotted spoon, leaving the juices behind, and transfer to a 20-cm/8-in deep, round baking dish.

Scatter the crumble over the apples and bake for about 30 minutes, or until the fruit is bubbling. Serve with custard, cream or ice cream.

CHOCOLATE, RUM AND RAISIN SOURDOUGH BREAD AND BUTTER PUDDING

This is such a treat served hot—but equally divine nibbled at, cold from the fridge if you're that kind of person. Make sure you use a sourdough with a bouncy soft crumb—not a heavy, dense one: you'll need a loaf that weighs the best part of 500g / 1lb 2oz. I've variously made this pudding with sourdough loaves made with white flour and rye, spelt and rye, and ale: all were lovely, and just made for cavorting in a baking dish with chocolate and custard. A splodge of custard over the top isn't absolutely necessary, but rather nice.

SERVES 6

1 Tbsp butter, for dotting, plus extra
  for greasing
75g/2¾oz raisins
90ml/3fl oz rum
375ml/12¾fl oz whole milk
90ml/3fl oz double [heavy] cream
2 tsp vanilla extract
3 large eggs
75g/2¾oz caster [superfine] sugar
finely grated zest of 1 orange

generous pinch of salt
about 400g/14oz sourdough bread (see
  note above), cut into 1-cm/⅜-in slices
200g/7oz chocolate hazelnut spread
40g/1½oz skinless hazelnuts, lightly
  toasted and roughly chopped
1 Tbsp demerara [light brown] sugar,
  for sprinkling
custard, cream or vanilla ice cream,
  to serve

Preheat the oven to 180°C/350°F/Gas mark 4 and butter an ovenproof dish, roughly 24 × 20cm/9½ × 8in.

Place the raisins in a small bowl, pour over the rum and set aside for 20 minutes. Drain and reserve the rum.

In a jug, mix the reserved rum with the milk, cream, vanilla, eggs, caster sugar, orange zest and salt.

Slather the bread with the chocolate spread. Arrange enough of the slices to cover the bottom of the prepared baking dish in a single layer, overlapping slightly, chocolate-side facing upwards. You might have to cut some of the slices into smaller pieces to fit. Scatter over the drained raisins and the hazelnuts, then pour over half the milk and egg mixture.

Add a second layer of bread, this time with the chocolate-side facing downwards. Pour over the remaining milk and egg mixture and press down gently with a spatula. Dot the 1 tablespoon of butter over the top and sprinkle with the demerara sugar. Bake for 25–30 minutes until puffed, golden and still a bit wobbly in the middle. Serve hot with custard, cream or vanilla ice cream.

CHOCOLATE, BANANA AND HAZELNUT GALETTE

Antony and Cleopatra. Meghan and Harry. Gin and tonic. Chocolate and banana. Some couplings are just meant to be. This is a quick and delicious dessert you can make from pantry ingredients. Perfect with a scoop of vanilla ice cream or a cloud of whipped cream on top.

SERVES 6

200g/7oz plain [all-purpose] flour
60g/2¼oz caster [superfine] sugar
50g/1¾oz ground hazelnuts
pinch of salt
125g/4½oz cold unsalted butter, chopped
2 egg yolks, lightly beaten

2 Tbsp runny honey
100g/3½oz dark chocolate (between 60–70% cocoa solids), roughly chopped
3 medium ripe bananas
1–2 Tbsp demerara [light brown] sugar, for sprinkling
1 egg, lightly beaten with a splash of milk, for egg wash

First, make your dough. Using a fork or balloon whisk, whisk the flour, caster sugar, ground hazelnuts and salt together in a bowl to combine. Transfer to a food processor, add the butter and pulse to a breadcrumb consistency. Add the egg yolks, a little at a time, pulsing between additions, to make a shaggy dough. Tip out onto a work surface, knead briefly and shape into a disc. Wrap in plastic wrap and chill for 30 minutes.

Meanwhile, preheat the oven to 180°C/350°F/Gas mark 4 and place a baking sheet inside to heat. Warm the honey in a small pan and set aside.

Roll out the dough between 2 pieces of baking paper into a circle roughly 35cm/14in in diameter. Carefully peel off the top layer of paper.

Using a bowl, plate or pan lid as a guide, mark out (but don't cut!) a circle roughly 22cm/8¾in in diameter in the centre of the dough. Using a sharp knife, cut out a circle 32cm/12½in in diameter around the marked-out circle: there should be a 5-cm/2-in border between the marked-out circle and the edge of the pastry.

Scatter the chopped chocolate within the border of the marked-out circle. Thinly slice the bananas and arrange neatly on top of the chocolate. Brush the bananas with the warmed honey and sprinkle with 1 tablespoon of the demerara sugar.

Fold the border inwards, pleating and gently pressing to form a neat edge as you go. Brush the dough with the egg wash and sprinkle with the remaining sugar. Quickly slide the galette on its paper onto the hot baking sheet and bake for 30 minutes until golden and crisp underneath. Serve immediately.

CHOCOLATE, MARMALADE AND GINGER STEAMED PUDDING

Chocolate and marmalade are a magnificent match in this traditional steamed pudding, made more delicious with the addition of nuggets of preserved ginger. The sponge itself is lovely and moist, and invested with a generous marmalade crown. But as it doesn't have rivers of sauce, it's best served with a jug of custard —ideally spiked with rum or whisky—alongside.

SERVES 6-8

175g/6oz unsalted butter, softened, plus extra for greasing
5 heaped Tbsp marmalade
50g/1¾oz/3 balls stem [preserved] ginger from a jar, chopped, plus 1–2 Tbsp syrup from the jar (if needed)
175g/6oz plain [all-purpose] flour
45g/1½oz cocoa powder
2 tsp baking powder
pinch of salt
175g/6oz caster [superfine] sugar
3 large eggs, lightly beaten
4–5 Tbsp milk
custard or ice cream, to serve

Generously grease a 1.2-litre/42-fl oz/1.3-quart pudding basin [ovenproof bowl] with butter and line the base with a circle of baking paper. Butter a large square of foil.

If your marmalade is very firm, stir in some of the stem ginger syrup: what you want is a loose mixture. Spoon the marmalade into the base of the pudding basin and set aside.

Using a fork or balloon whisk, whisk the flour, cocoa, baking powder and salt together in a bowl.

In a mixing bowl or the bowl of a stand mixer, beat the butter and sugar together until pale and fluffy. Gradually beat in the eggs, adding a little of the flour mixture if it starts to curdle. Stir in the flour mixture and enough of the milk to form a soft dropping consistency. Fold in the chopped stem ginger.

Spoon the mixture into the basin and smooth the top. Make 2 pleats in the centre of the prepared foil, place buttered-side down and secure with string around the rim. Place an upturned saucer in a large pan and place the basin on top. Pour in enough boiling water to come one-quarter way up the side of the basin. Cover with a lid and simmer for 1¾ hours, topping up with more boiling water if necessary.

Carefully remove the basin from the pan, run a knife around the sides to loosen and invert onto a plate. Serve with custard or ice cream.

CHOCOLATE-SWIRL PAVLOVA WITH ROASTED RHUBARB AND CACAO NIB CREAM

Australia and New Zealand may bicker over where pavlova was invented, but it certainly played a starring role in celebratory meals when I was growing up in Sydney. This version of the classic meringue-topped-with-fruit-and-cream dessert is gloriously gooey and, to be honest, a little messy. The crisp meringue conceals a decadent heart of oozing chocolate, and the rhubarb provides a tangy counterpoint to all the richness.

SERVES 6
150g/5¼oz dark chocolate (70% cocoa solids), finely chopped
4 large egg whites
200g/7oz caster [superfine] sugar
¼ tsp fine sea salt

FOR THE CREAM
300ml/10fl oz double [heavy] cream
2 Tbsp cacao nibs

FOR THE RHUBARB
250g/8¾oz rhubarb, cut into thumb-sized pieces
40g/1½oz caster [superfine] sugar

Preheat the oven to 120°C/250°F/Gas mark ½. On a sheet of baking paper, mark out a circle roughly 20cm/8in in diameter using a plate or pan lid as a guide. Place on a baking sheet and set aside.

Melt the chocolate in a heatproof bowl set over a pan of barely simmering water, making sure the bottom of the bowl doesn't touch the water. Remove the bowl from the pan and set aside to cool to lukewarm or room temperature.

In a scrupulously clean bowl with electric beaters or in a stand mixer, whisk the egg whites to stiff peaks. Gradually add the sugar and salt, beating constantly, until thick and glossy. It's crucial that the mixture is very stiff.

Pour the cooled chocolate over the meringue—don't stir or beat it in. Scoop the mixture into the circle marked out on the baking paper to make a neat round, retaining some swirls of chocolate in the meringue. Bake for 1 hour 15 minutes until crisp on the outside.

Meanwhile, make the cacao nib cream. Pour 120ml/4fl oz of the cream into a small pan and add the cacao nibs. Bring almost to the boil, then remove the pan from the heat and set aside to infuse and cool.

When the meringue is cooked, remove from the oven and leave to cool. Increase the oven temperature to 200°C/400°F/Gas mark 6. Place the rhubarb pieces in a baking dish, add the sugar and toss together, then spread out in a single layer. Cover with foil and roast for 15 minutes, then remove the foil and cook for a further 5 minutes, or until the rhubarb is tender but still holding its shape. Remove from the oven and leave to cool.

Strain the cooled infused cream and discard the nibs. Whip the remaining cream until it barely holds its shape, then stir in the infused cream.

To assemble the pavlova, top the meringue with the cream and then the rhubarb and any pan juices, and serve immediately.

POACHED NECTARINES IN MUSCAT AND
NIB SYRUP WITH TONKA BEAN CREAM

This is a chic and simple dessert, perfect for a summer lunch in the garden. It's not only very simple to prepare, but it has to be made ahead and chilled, thereby removing the need for any last-minute dessert faffing. The nibs lend a very gentle hint of cocoa—like a faint melody carried on the breeze—and no chocolate richness at all. This is a terrific example of how cocoa can be used subtly, like a spice, in sweet dishes.

SERVES 4

4 ripe nectarines
200g/7oz caster [superfine] sugar
200ml/6¾fl oz Muscat
2 tsp cacao nibs
juice of 1 lemon
100ml/3½fl oz water
1 handful of basil leaves, for sprinkling

FOR THE MASCARPONE CREAM

125g/4½oz mascarpone cheese
100g/3½oz Greek yogurt
½–1 tonka bean, grated, or seeds from
  1 vanilla pod [bean]
2 Tbsp icing [confectioners'] sugar

Place the nectarines in a heatproof bowl, cover with just-boiled water and leave for 10 seconds. Drain, cover with cold water, then peel off the skins. Cut the fruit in half and carefully remove the stones, trying not to damage the flesh. Set aside.

Place the sugar, Muscat, cacao nibs, lemon juice and water in a pan large enough to fit the nectarines snugly in a single layer. Set the pan over a medium-high heat and cook for 3–5 minutes, stirring constantly, until the sugar dissolves.

Remove the pan from the heat and add the nectarine halves, cut-side down. Return to the heat and simmer for 3 minutes, spooning some of the syrup over the fruit as they cook. Carefully transfer the fruit and syrup to a bowl and leave to cool to room temperature, then chill.

Meanwhile, make the mascarpone cream by mixing all the ingredients together in a bowl. Chill for at least 2 hours, or until needed.

To serve, distribute the nectarines among bowls, generously spoon over the syrup and top with the mascarpone cream. Sprinkle with basil leaves and serve immediately.

In Australia when I was a kid, every trip to the cinema involved the purchase of a choc top: a cone filled with vanilla ice cream and enrobed in a shell of hard dark chocolate. That first bite through the shell into the ice cream was always a bit of a killer — tooth pain *and* brain freeze — but always worth the pain. This is my version: a tangy mango ice cream with a dark chocolate sauce that 'magically' hardens when it hits the ice cream. For me, this is happiness in a cone.

MAKES 8–12 CONES (1.2 LITRES / 40FL OZ ICE CREAM)

1.1kg/2½lb ripe mango flesh, ideally
   Alphonso mangoes (canned or frozen
   mango pieces also work well)
80g/2¾oz icing [confectioners'] sugar
pinch of salt
2 Tbsp lime juice

120ml/4fl oz double [heavy] cream
ice cream cones, to serve

FOR THE MAGIC CHOCOLATE SAUCE

240g/8½oz dark chocolate (70%
   cocoa solids), chopped
2 Tbsp coconut oil (about 30g/1oz)

Place all the ingredients for the ice cream in a blender and blitz until smooth. Have a taste: it should be quite sweet and also a little tangy from the lime juice. The balance will depend on the sweetness of your mangoes, so add more sugar if necessary. Chill for 2 hours, then churn in an ice-cream maker according to the manufacturer's instructions.

When you are ready to serve, make the sauce. Melt the chocolate and coconut oil together in a heatproof bowl set over a pan of barely simmering water, making sure the bottom of the bowl doesn't touch the water. Stir to combine, then remove the bowl from the pan and leave to cool a little.

Scoop some ice cream into the cones, pressing it in firmly, then carefully and quickly dip the ice cream into the chocolate sauce — and enjoy watching it harden.

Eating ice cream will always make me think of being in Sicily, sitting at a pavement table at Caffe Sicilia, in the gorgeous Baroque city of Noto, talking to gelato genius Corrado Assenza. The fourth generation co-owner took the time to chat to me about his world-renowned gelato and granita, which he makes fresh every day using the finest seasonal Sicilian nuts, fruits, vegetables and herbs. Corrado plied me with different flavours—strawberry and tomato, chocolate, pistachio and almond—into which I dipped his freshly made, ethereally light brioche rolls. Reader, I made a pig of myself. Truly.

It seems odd that frozen desserts were probably invented in southern Italy in the seventeenth century in the intense Mediterranean heat. How they prevented it from melting into puddles at the lavish feasts where it was served is a puzzle: they must have eaten very quickly. Chocolate ice cream was born, or at least recorded, in 1794, when Neapolitan Vincenzo Corrado published a long treatise on chocolate, which included a recipe for sorbet. The instructions involve making a ganache from chocolate, water, sugar and vanilla, then freezing it in snow layered with salt. (The salt lowers the freezing point of the ice.)

The freezing technology might have improved over the centuries, but according to Corrado, his own recipe for chocolate gelato is very simple. "I make a ganache with milk, sugar and 100% chocolate, and then use a gelato machine," he says. That's it? I ask. "Nothing more," he laughs. "There's no secret."

This recipe is inspired by the bowlful of chocolate granita I ate at Caffe Sicilia (you will have to go to Noto yourself to sample his exact recipe). Use the highest quality 100% chocolate you can afford, because it's the key to the success of this gelato. I used Willie's Cacao 100% Peruvian Black chocolate to develop and test this recipe; the distinctive notes of juicy raisins delivered an absolutely intense and gorgeous gelato.

MAKES ABOUT 800G / 1¾LB
OR ALMOST 1 LITRE / 33¾FL OZ
200g/7oz dark chocolate (100% cocoa
  solids), finely chopped or grated
500ml/17fl oz whole milk
250g/8¾oz caster [superfine] sugar

Have the chopped chocolate in a large heatproof jug by the hob [stove].

Place the milk and sugar in a pan and simmer until the sugar has completely dissolved. Immediately pour the milk over the chocolate, whisking constantly until melted, thick and glossy. Set aside until it cools to room temperature, then chill until cold.

Pour the cold mixture into a blender and blitz to ensure there are no lumps or crystals, then transfer to an ice-cream maker and churn according to the manufacturer's instructions.

Delicious served sandwiched in a brioche roll.

DUCK FAT CARAMEL AND CHOCOLATE BAY LEAF TART

Banish any notion that this tart tastes like it should form part of the roast dinner instead of the pudding. Using duck fat instead of butter in the caramel imbues all that sweetness with a subtly savoury richness. I've also made this with goose fat, with excellent results. When it comes to how much salt to use in the caramel, that really depends on your personal taste: start with the amount suggested and add more if you like.

SERVES 8

FOR THE PASTRY
200g/7oz plain [all-purpose] flour,
  plus extra for dusting
100g/3½oz cold unsalted butter, diced
50g/1¾oz icing [confectioners'] sugar
generous pinch of fine sea salt
2 large egg yolks, lightly beaten

FOR THE CARAMEL
260ml/8¾fl oz double [heavy] cream
60g/2¼oz duck fat
270g/9½oz caster [superfine] sugar
75ml/2½oz maple syrup
1 heaped tsp sea salt flakes, or more
  to taste
50ml/1⅔fl oz water

FOR THE CHOCOLATE GANACHE
250g/8¾oz dark chocolate (60% cocoa
  solids), grated or finely blitzed in a
  food processor
200ml/6¾fl oz double [heavy] cream
1 Tbsp liquid glucose
3 bay leaves
sea salt flakes, for sprinkling

First, make the pastry. Place the flour, butter, icing sugar and salt in a food processor and pulse to a fine breadcrumb consistency. Gradually add the egg yolks, pulsing between each addition, to make a shaggy dough. Tip out onto a work surface, shape into a disc and wrap in plastic wrap. Chill for at least 1 hour.

On a lightly floured work surface, roll the pastry out into a circle large enough to line a 24-cm/9½-in tart tin. Line the tin with the dough: use a ball of excess dough dipped in flour to press it into the fluted sides and to make a neat crease between the edges and base. Gently push some of the excess pastry hanging over the edge of the tin back into the tin—this will allow for shrinkage in the oven. Don't worry if the pastry tears; just patch it up with excess bits of dough. Run a rolling pin over the rim of the tart tin to trim, and pull away any excess pastry. Prick the base with a fork and chill for 20 minutes. Meanwhile, preheat the oven to 170°C/340°F/Gas mark 3.

Line the pastry case with baking paper—scrunch it up and then unscrunch it to make it easier—and fill with baking beans or rice. Bake for 15 minutes. Remove the paper and the beans, then bake for a further 10 minutes until pale gold. Leave to cool in the tin.

Now, make the caramel. Place the cream and duck fat in a small pan and gently heat until the fat has melted. Remove the pan from the heat and set aside.

Place the caster sugar, maple syrup and salt in a pan with the water and stir to combine. Simmer until the mixture turns a deep amber colour (or until the temperature reaches 150°C/302°F on a sugar thermometer). Remove the pan from the heat and whisk in the cream and duck fat mixture — be careful, as it will splutter. Return the pan to the heat and gently simmer, stirring constantly (I use a whisk), until very thick and a rich caramel colour. Pour into the tart case and set aside at room temperature to cool and set, 1–2 hours.

To make the ganache, place the chocolate in a heatproof bowl. Place the cream, liquid glucose and bay leaves in a small pan, bring almost to the boil and then remove from the heat. Set aside to infuse for 30 minutes. Remove the bay leaves and reheat until very hot, then immediately pour over the grated chocolate, stirring constantly. Whisk with a balloon whisk or electric beaters until thick and creamy. Spread over the caramel and smooth the top. Sprinkle with sea salt flakes. Serve immediately or leave to set at room temperature for 2 hours.

RYE, CHOCOLATE AND MACADAMIA RICOTTA CHEESECAKE WITH PX SHERRY RAISIN SAUCE

To my mind, this is a grown-up cheesecake with its layers of flavour and splosh of booze. The chocolate is in the base and not the filling, as is usual in chocolate cheesecakes, with the nibs providing some welcome texture and crunch.

SERVES 8–12

FOR THE BASE
3 Tbsp unsalted butter, melted,
  plus extra for greasing
90g/3¼oz rye flakes or oats
45g/1½oz macadamia nuts
45g/1½oz soft dark brown sugar
2 Tbsp cocoa powder
1½ Tbsp cacao nibs
¼ tsp sea salt flakes

FOR THE FILLING
270g/9½oz whole cream cheese
300g/10½oz ricotta cheese

130g/4½oz caster [superfine] sugar
3 large eggs
1 tsp vanilla extract
finely grated zest of ½ lemon
150ml/5fl oz double [heavy] cream

FOR THE SAUCE
90g/3¼oz raisins
75ml/2½fl oz Pedro Ximénez sherry
150g/5¼oz soft dark brown sugar
¼ tsp allspice
pinch of salt
strip of lemon peel
90ml/3fl oz water

Preheat the oven to 180°C/350°F/Gas mark 4. Butter a 20-cm/8-in round loose-bottomed or springform cake tin and wrap in foil to prevent water getting in.

Start by making the base. Lightly toast the rye flakes and macadamia nuts separately in a dry frying pan until lightly golden and toasty. Tip into a food processor and add the remaining base ingredients except the butter. Blitz to a rubble. Add the butter and blitz again until well combined. Tip the mixture into the cake tin, press down firmly with the back of a spoon and chill for 30 minutes.

For the filling, place the cream cheese, ricotta and sugar in a bowl and beat to combine. Beat in the eggs, vanilla and lemon zest until light and creamy. In a separate bowl, whip the cream to soft peaks. Fold into the cheese mixture, trying not to lose any of the air. Scrape into the cake tin and smooth the top. Place the tin in a roasting tray and fill with boiling water halfway up the side of the cake tin. Bake for 50 minutes, or until the top is firm but still has some wobble. Cool in the tin for 10 minutes, then run a hot knife around the edge to release the cheesecake.

Meanwhile, make the sauce. Soak the raisins in the sherry for 15 minutes. Put the sugar, allspice, salt, lemon peel and water in a pan and simmer for 5 minutes until starting to thicken. Add the raisins and soaking liquor and simmer until syrupy. Leave to cool. To serve, pour the syrup over and cut the cheesecake into slices.

FIG AND FRANGIPANE CROUSTADES WITH
COCOA AND LAPSANG SOUCHONG SYRUP

This elegant dessert is based on a recipe in Tamasin Day-Lewis's excellent cookbook *The Art of the Tart*. In her version, Tamasin uses pipe tobacco in the syrup, but I've opted for the smoky notes of lapsang souchong tea instead. It works a treat, turning a simple tart into something exceptional.

SERVES 6

8 large sheets filo [phyllo] pastry, each sheet measuring roughly 30 × 38cm/12 × 15in
60g/2¼oz unsalted butter, melted
6 ripe purple figs
caster [superfine] sugar, for sprinkling
cream of your choice, to serve

FOR THE FRANGIPANE

40g/1½oz caster [superfine] sugar
20g/¾oz ground almonds
½ tsp cornflour [cornstarch]
40g/1½oz unsalted butter, softened

FOR THE SYRUP

150ml/5fl oz freshly boiled water
1 lapsang souchong teabag
50g/1¾oz caster [superfine] sugar
1 Tbsp cocoa powder

Preheat the oven to 190°C/375°F/Gas mark 5 and line a baking sheet with baking paper.

First, make the frangipane. Mix all the ingredients together in a bowl to make a paste and set aside.

Lightly brush the filo sheets with the melted butter, stacking them on top of each other as you go. Cut out 6 × 10-cm/4-in circles from the stack using a small bowl as a guide. Transfer to the prepared baking sheet, buttered-side up.

Place about 1 tablespoon of frangipane on each filo circle and spread out, making sure to leave a 1-cm/⅜-in border. Thinly slice the figs and arrange, overlapping slightly, on the frangipane, then sprinkle with sugar. Bake for 15–20 minutes until the filo is golden, the bottom crisp and the figs tender.

Meanwhile, make the syrup. Pour the freshly boiled water into a cup, add the teabag and infuse for 2 minutes. Remove and reserve the teabag, then pour the tea into a small pan. Add the sugar and simmer until dissolved, then whisk in the cocoa. Simmer for 7–8 minutes until reduced and thickened to a thin syrup. Have a taste, and if it's lacking lapsang souchong flavour, remove the pan from the heat, pop the teabag in and infuse some more.

Serve the croustades hot with the syrup poured over and some cream on the side.

COCOA: AND THE ROLE OF WOMEN

"Obey that urge! Do you know that when you get an urge to eat chocolate, you shouldn't resist—there's a deep physical reason for it?"—Aero Milk Chocolate newspaper advertisement, 1938

I clearly remember an advertisement for Cherry Ripe chocolate bars that appeared on Australian television when I was a teenager in the early 1980s. A pretty lady dressed in white sat on a park bench eating a chocolate bar while a handsome male stranger next to her magically transformed a bag of cherries into a pink dove. The lady then gave the man a Cherry Ripe bar and they enjoyed eating the chocolate together, before nestling in each other's arms to watch a bright red sunset. As much as I loved Cherry Ripe, this all seemed very odd. Why did the woman have such an ecstatic look on her face as she took a bite? How did eating a Cherry Ripe land her a boyfriend? Why did the voiceover woman speak in such breathless tones?

I now know that if we trace its sticky history back to the beginning, chocolate advertising has long been intertwined with women and sex, and generally marketed to consumers as 'Female Food'. From the suggestive Cherry Ripe advert—Australia's version of the UK's quasi-erotic Cadbury's Flake commercials—right back to eighteenth-century posters urging mothers to nourish their children with cocoa drinks, chocolate has been presented to consumers as particularly feminine, but why?

It's true that women and chocolate have always been deeply connected. In Mesoamerican times, female hands ground the cacao beans to make drinks for the elite, and in the early days of mass-produced chocolate it fell to women in the factories to decorate the confectionery prettily and assemble the charming assortment boxes. Today, women still play a key (and often unacknowledged) role in cacao production, particularly in West Africa. But this doesn't explain why women continue to be depicted in adverts lolling about, suggestively gorging on bars like mad chocoholics.

It might stem back to chocolate's very early associations with 'bad' women. In the seventeenth century, after Spanish settlers in the New World acquired a taste for chocolate, women rather than men began to be accused of not being able to control their cocoa cravings. In his book, *Travels in the New World* (1648), English Dominican friar Thomas Gage tells the story of a new bishop in the Mexican city Chiapas who threatened to excommunicate a group of upper-class Spanish women if they continued to drink hot chocolate during mass. The women insisted they needed the drink for sustenance and to settle their weak stomachs, while the bishop argued it disrupted proceedings. In the end, the women ignored his threats of excommunication and chose chocolate over hellfire. The bishop? He died, apparently from drinking a cup of poisoned chocolate.

It's one of numerous stories that involve women accused of using chocolate for nefarious purposes, including witchcraft. Many testimonies from the Spanish Inquisition hearings in New Spain (parts of the Americas then controlled by Spain) concerned native and 'mulatto' women who were said to have mixed chocolate with (often vile) ingredients for the purposes of sorcery. According to the accounts, these 'witches' were often hired by upper-class Spanish women to solve various problems. They concocted a chocolate potion that included menstrual blood to seduce a man, or the heart of a crow and human excrement to make a lover fall out of love with his wife. One example from 1620 concerns the addition of human flesh to chocolate — but is frustratingly silent on the intended recipient or purpose of the drink.

"Don Baltasar Pena said... he had found under the bed of one of the mulatto women that served in his household a piece of flesh taken from the quarter of a man that had been hanged, and that she has roasted it and then mixed with chocolate."

Chocolate was the perfect vehicle for these additives. Readily available and widely offered as a token of hospitality, the drink's bitterness and thick texture could easily disguise even the foulest flavours.

Eighteenth-century doctors blamed chocolate for the 'disease' of 'hysteria' they claimed was rife among women in the cities of Mexico and Puebla, particularly nuns. Chocolate had become a staple in religious orders by this time and nuns enjoyed a life of relative luxury, thanks to the wealth amassed by the convents. They could afford to drink liberal quantities of chocolate, which was prepared by their servants and served to them in the privacy of their quarters. So, their love of the drink was blamed for their so-called malady. (Modern researchers suggest the 'hysteria' might not have been caused by the over-consumption of chocolate at all. Regulations introduced at the end of the eighteenth century forced the nuns to eat communally, which saw their chocolate intake fall. Was it the slump in chocolate consumption that triggered anxiety?)

By the mid-seventeenth century, chocolate was consumed by powerful rich men in parlours and coffee houses in the major cities of Western Europe. But its reputation as the preferred drink of idle women seeped over from New Spain, reinforced by upper-class women who adopted it as their drink of choice and often enjoyed it in the comfort of their beds. In the late seventeenth century, King William III and Queen Mary II took their chocolate during a bedroom ceremony known as the 'levée', when they would dress in front of a chosen few. And paintings like *The Morning Chocolate*, by Venetian artist Pietro Longhi (c.1750), portrays a woman enjoying her chocolate propped up on pillows in bed, surrounded by a retinue of servants and a well-dressed man. This depiction of a reclining woman indulgently consuming chocolate is not a million miles removed from modern adverts featuring women lazing around on the sofa or in the bath, nibbling pleasurably and indulgently on a bar.

In the nineteenth century, the nexus between women and chocolate split into two paths: one maternal and domestic, and the other romantic and sexual.

THE POWER OF ADVERTISING

Thanks to the Industrial Revolution, cocoa could be produced relatively cheaply and on a mass scale, so chocolate drinks were no longer the preserve of the rich and elite. Drawing on chocolate's longstanding reputation as a healthful, even medicinal food, manufacturers linked cocoa to a domestic version of femininity, and the Victorian notion that the family formed the moral heart of the nation. Posters advertising cocoa depicted mothers bonding with their happy children over steaming mugs. The message was clear: good mothers nourished their families by giving them wholesome treats. The invention of milk chocolate further strengthened the link between cocoa and nurturing in advertising. In the 1930s,

British chocolate manufacturer Rowntree's introduced its 'special mothers' campaign: 'For growing children, there's no better drink at mealtimes', read one caption.

Chocolate advertising reflected women's place in society. Many women worked outside the home during the Second World War, but when it ended they were expected to return to the domestic sphere. Reflecting this, housewives began to star in chocolate advertising of the 1940s and 1950s, says historian Emma Robertson, in her book *Chocolate, Women and Empire* (2013). Savvy housewives bought cocoa in pursuit of domestic perfection, the ads implied. In a late 1940s Rowntree® campaign, 'My Wife's a Witch', a woman performs housewifely miracles thanks to Rowntree's cocoa. Her grateful husband responds: "I picked her for her eyelashes—I never dreamt she was so wizard at housekeeping. D'you wonder I'm spellbound." This curious, unnerving campaign, harked back to the centuries-old association between chocolate, women and witchcraft.

We can probably blame the mass production of boxed assortments for women being presented as sexual objects in chocolate advertising. Cadbury launched Milk Tray in 1915, the first widely affordable box of chocolates in the UK; ideal as a gift, these assortments were soon aligned with heterosexual romance, sexuality and desire. Rowntree's recovered from near financial ruin thanks to its 'letters' campaign, which positioned its Black Magic assortment (a name that combined a bizarre mix of the romantic and the occult) as a luxurious treat with which men could woo white, heterosexual, sophisticated ladies. The ads depicted women writing intimate letters to each other about receiving Black Magic from romantic prospects. One of the most explicit, from 1934, almost portrays women as idiotic chocolate obsessives: "We silly creatures are always so thrilled when a man thinks us worth the very best. Imagine it, a big box of these new Black Magic chocolates on my dressing table. My dear, each choc's an orgy." Up until the 1950s, the adverts conveyed the message that men who gave women Black Magic were an excellent catch.

Manufacturers assumed that women were such chocoholics that a strawberry cream or two was enough to win them over. In 1936, after decades of being outwitted by Cadbury's campaigns, Rowntree's launched its Dairy Box chocolate assortment. Designed to be given to women but marketed at men, an early slogan was: 'She'll love it if you bring her chocolates, She'll love you if they're Dairy Box.' This was one in a string of chocolate adverts that implied that a boxed assortment was sufficient reason for a woman to go out with a man. Moreover, some ads implied that sexual reward was a given: 'For Dairy Box I'll give you a kiss', one catchline read.

Shifting moral values in the 1960s and more liberal attitudes to sex sharpened the focus on women as sexual objects. Chocolate advertising turned risqué, with the highly suggestive Cadbury's Flake television commercials the most provocative of them all. These depicted women variously escaping to the bath, skipping through the countryside or ignoring a ringing telephone in order to enjoy a moment's selfish pleasure with a chocolate bar. They opened the Flake wrapper suggestively and took a feminine bite, whereupon they closed their eyes in pleasure.

Dave Trott, the advertising guru behind some of the Flake ads, confirmed to Britain's *Stylist* magazine that the allusion in the advertisement to women having orgasms was intended. "Nothing is allowed to interrupt that delicious, orgasmic moment of self-indulgence," he said. In the same article, a spokesperson for Cadbury insisted, apparently straight-faced, that although the ads were loved by men, they were actually aimed at women.

Today, drumming gorillas, crazy-eyebrowed children and ambassadors' receptions feature in chocolate advertising, but the ladies are still there, too. Godiva is a master of the art of the chocolate = sexy woman trope. Its sensual 2017 campaign for the Masterpieces line featured conventionally beautiful women drenched in melted chocolate, along with close-up shots of their lipsticked mouths holding a square between their teeth. Lindt's advertisement for Lindor truffles is also the stuff of another era: a woman in comfy socks and jumper relaxes on the sofa, seductively eating a chocolate, eyes closed in pleasure. Cadbury recently re-introduced the 'Milk Tray Man' ads, which first appeared on British television in 1968. These feature a James Bond-style action man dressed in black overcoming danger to deliver a box of Milk Tray to a beautiful woman, 'All because the lady loves Milk Tray'.

Is it possible that advertising reflects a fundamental truth that women are somehow biologically hardwired to love chocolate more than men? I don't think so. Some studies do show a link between gender and food preferences, with red meat appealing to men, and lighter foods and sweets speaking to women. Some experts say evolution explains this: men were the hunters who dragged home meaty protein, while women, who gathered fruit and vegetables, developed a sweet tooth. Really?

A famous US study found that nearly half of American women regularly craved chocolate, compared to just 20 per cent of men. Was it something to do with their hormones? Was there a physiological reason chocolate soothed premenstrual syndrome and heartbreak? No. The study showed that outside the US, the situation was different. In Spain, men and women hankered after chocolate equally, while in Egypt, both genders actually preferred salty food. I think the supposedly female desire for chocolate is just a stereotype reinforced — and exacerbated — by marketing.

Food manufacturers often focus their marketing on women's guilt about eating, a truth underscored in adverts that show women consuming chocolate in private, away from judgemental eyes. As early as 1698, chocolate was blamed for making Parisian women fat. "Why do Parisians, especially the women, become so corpulent?" puzzled Dr Martin Lister in his *Journey to Paris in the Year 1698* (2011). It was partly due, he concluded, to their daily intake of chocolate.

It's really no surprise that in recent years, manufacturers have come up with new chocolate products — low-fat, low-calorie, low-sugar — that tap into women's anxieties about their appearance. One expensive bar launched in the last few years even claims to protect women's skin from ageing and contribute to its radiant appearance. "All the lady things rolled into one," as one reviewer observed drily. Chocolate's association with womanhood lives on.

A MELTING MOUTHFUL

It's hard to think of a more universally adored American culinary classic than chocolate chip cookies — or one more fiercely debated when it comes to the 'perfect' version. Chewy or crisp? Thick or thin? Chocolate chips or gooey chunks? Galaxies of internet space are devoted to forensic explorations of the science behind chocolate chip cookie excellence, and countless recipes lay claim to be the 'ultimate'.

The inventor of this outrageously good chocolate-spiked morsel would no doubt be pleased but bemused by it all. Ruth Graves Wakefield, owner of the Toll House Inn in Whitman, Massachusetts, came up with her Toll House Chocolate Crunch Cookies recipe in the late 1930s. Theories abound about its genesis. One has it that she ran out of nuts for her regular cookie recipe and replaced them with chunks chopped from a bar of Nestlé chocolate. Another unlikely legend states that a jar of chocolate pieces mistakenly fell into a vat of cookie dough as it was being mixed. According to cookie scholar Carolyn Wyman, the truth is more prosaic. Wakefield devised them "by dint of training, talent, [and] hard work," she writes in *The Great American Chocolate Chip Cookie Book*.

Whatever the truth, Wakefield first published the recipe for Toll House cookies in the 1938 edition of her cookbook *Toll House Tried and True Recipes*. Requiring relatively basic ingredients, the cookies were simple to bake and deliciously comforting served warm from the oven. In short, they were the perfect antidote to the Depression and an immediate hit. The rest is history.

Wakefield tweaked the recipe herself over the years, and infinite hybrids have sprouted up and been enjoyed all over the planet. Here's mine: banana, tahini and chocolate make an outrageously tasty combination.

MAKES ABOUT 28 COOKIES

150g/5¼oz unsalted butter

120g/4¼oz plain [all-purpose] flour

120g/4¼oz spelt flour

¾ tsp baking powder

½ tsp bicarbonate of soda [baking soda]

½ tsp fine sea salt

280g/10oz dark chocolate (70% cocoa solids), roughly chopped, with some biggish chunks and some small bits

1 very ripe banana, about 100g/3½oz without skin

1 large egg

220g/7¾oz soft light brown sugar

40g/1½oz granulated sugar

1 tsp vanilla extract

80g/2¾oz tahini (must be smooth and runny enough to run off a spoon easily)

flaked sea salt or fleur de sel, for sprinkling

Place the butter in a heavy, light-coloured pan and melt over a medium-high heat, swirling frequently, until the butter smells gorgeously nutty and has turned dark brown. Remove from the heat and transfer to a mixing bowl or the bowl of a stand mixer, making sure you scrape in all the brown bits from the bottom of the pan (this is flavour!). Leave to cool for at least 5 minutes.

Meanwhile, using a fork or balloon whisk, whisk the flours, baking powder, bicarbonate of soda and salt together in a bowl to combine. Add the chopped chocolate and stir to evenly distribute.

In a small bowl, mash the banana until smooth, then add to the cooled butter, along with the egg, both the sugars, vanilla and tahini. Whisk for a good 5 minutes until creamy and much paler than when you started—this is a sign the mixture has aerated well.

Fold in the flour and chocolate mixture in 2 additions. Don't overmix or beat smooth: dough with an uneven consistency delivers welcome texture to the baked cookies. Chill for at least 2 hours.

Preheat the oven to 170°C/340°F/Gas mark 3 and line a large baking sheet with baking paper (you will need to cook these in batches). Scoop heaped tablespoons of dough onto the prepared baking sheet (about 40–45g/1½–1¾oz each), leaving at least 5cm/2in between them. Bake for 6 minutes, then turn the baking sheet round and bake for a further 6 minutes or so until brown at the edges (the centre might look a little undercooked but it's not).

Lightly sprinkle the cookies with the flaked salt while still warm. Leave on the baking sheet for 5 minutes, then transfer to a wire rack to cool.

CHOCOLATE, OLIVE OIL AND ROSEMARY COOKIES WITH ALMONDS

Dark chocolate and olive oil is a winning combination. They have many flavour notes in common—floral, grass and pepper, just to name a few—and can therefore sing together in subtle harmony. Olive oil chocolate cake is a classic and an increasingly popular example of how they work together beautifully. Here, I've paired dark chocolate with olive oil in cookies with equally delicious results. A chocolate cookie for grown-ups.

MAKES 18 COOKIES

140g/5oz plain [all-purpose] flour
20g/¾oz cocoa powder
1 tsp finely chopped rosemary
¾ tsp bicarbonate of soda [baking soda]
¼ tsp sea salt flakes, plus more
   for sprinkling

60ml/2fl oz extra virgin olive oil
120g/4¼oz soft light brown sugar
1 large egg
120g/4¼oz dark chocolate (between
   60–70% cocoa solids), roughly chopped
20g/¾oz blanched almonds,
   roughly chopped

Preheat the oven to 180°C/350°F/Gas mark 4 and line 1 large or 2 small baking sheets with baking paper.

Using a fork or balloon whisk, whisk the flour, cocoa powder, rosemary, bicarbonate of soda and salt together in a bowl.

Beat the oil, sugar and egg together in a stand mixer or in a bowl with electric beaters until creamy. You want to try to get as much air into the mixture as possible, so beat for a good 5 minutes. Mix in the flour mixture and then half the chopped chocolate. Chill for 1 hour to firm up.

Scoop out pieces of dough, about the size of large walnuts, and roll into balls —use damp/wet hands, as the mixture is quite wet. Transfer to the prepared baking sheets, leaving about 5cm/2in between each ball. Flatten the balls slightly with your palm to make 6-cm/2½-in circles. Top with the remaining chocolate and the almonds.

Bake for about 12 minutes, turning the sheet/s halfway through. Remove from the oven and leave for a few minutes, then transfer to a wire rack to cool completely.

CHOCOLATE-DIPPED ORANGE AND CARAWAY SHORTBREAD

Shortbread, generally, is delicious in its plain simplicity, but in this version, caraway adds vibrant flavour. It can be a pungent spice with a strong earthy taste and notes of anise, black pepper and citrus, but used with a light hand as it is here, it lends a gentle perfume to the soft buttery shortbread, and chimes beautifully with the orange zest. It also teases out the cocoa flavours in the milk chocolate—very moreish.

MAKES 12 SHORTBREADS

335g/11¾oz unsalted butter, at room
  temperature
finely grated zest of 2 large oranges
120g/4¼oz icing [confectioners'] sugar
300g/10½oz plain [all-purpose] flour

75g/2¾oz cornflour [cornstarch]
3 tsp caraway seeds
generous ¼ tsp fine sea salt
300g/10½oz milk chocolate, finely
  chopped

Preheat the oven to 150°C/300°F/Gas mark 2. Line the base and sides of a 20 × 20-cm/8 × 8-in brownie tray or baking dish with baking paper, cutting slits in each corner so it fits neatly. Let the paper hang over the edges so you can use it as handles to lift the cooked shortbread out of the tray.

Beat the butter and orange zest together in a stand mixer or in a bowl with electric beaters until pale and creamy—this will take a good 5 minutes. Gradually beat in the icing sugar.

In a separate bowl, using a fork or balloon whisk, whisk both flours, the caraway seeds and salt together. Add to the butter mixture and beat on low speed until the flour is only just combined. Don't overbeat or the shortbread will be tough. Press the mixture evenly into the prepared tray and bake for 50–55 minutes until firm and the palest gold. Leave in the tray to cool completely.

When cool, lift out onto a chopping [cutting] board. You can cut the shortbread into whatever size pieces you like, but this is the way I like to do it. Using a serrated knife, slice the shortbread square in half and then cut each half into 6 fingers, roughly 10 × 3cm/4 × 1¼in. The pieces might crumble, but this is the nature of shortbread—we're not aiming for diamond-cut edges here. Transfer to a wire rack set over a rimmed baking sheet or board.

Melt the chocolate in a heatproof bowl set over a bowl of barely simmering water, making sure the bottom of the bowl doesn't touch the water. (Alternatively, melt the chocolate while keeping it in temper using the hairdryer method on page 43.) Spoon the chocolate over half of each shortbread finger. Set for at least 1 hour.

RYE CHOCOLATE BROWNIE AND PEANUT BUTTER COOKIE SANDWICHES

The genius behind Reese's Peanut Butter Cups was one Harry Burnett (H.B.) Reese, a former employee of US chocolate scion Milton S. Hershey. Reese set out to make his own name in the candy business in the 1920s and his peanut butter chocolate bites were an immediate hit. Little wonder really, at least to those of us for whom these morsels are catnip: the sweetened peanut butter nestled in a chocolate case embodies the holy trinity of fat, sugar and salt. The circle was squared when Hershey bought the company for more than $US23 million in the early 1960s, and Reese was posthumously inducted into the American Candy Hall of Fame in 2009 (fantastic—but what took them so long?). I have developed these luscious cookie sandwiches in his honour.

MAKES 16 SANDWICHES

FOR THE COOKIES

120g/4¼oz unsalted butter,
  at room temperature
180g/6oz soft light brown sugar
1 large egg, lightly beaten
1 tsp vanilla extract
125g/4½oz cocoa powder
35g/1¼oz plain [all-purpose] flour
35g/1¼oz rye flour
½ tsp bicarbonate of soda [baking soda]
½ tsp fine sea salt

FOR THE FILLING

130g/4½oz smooth peanut butter
2 Tbsp unsalted butter
40g/1½oz icing [confectioners']
  sugar, sifted
pinch of salt, if needed

Preheat the oven to 160°C/325°F/Gas mark 3 and line a large baking sheet with baking paper. You will probably have to cook these in a couple of batches.

Beat the butter and sugar together in a stand mixer or in a bowl with electric beaters until pale and creamy—this will take a good 5 minutes. Gradually add the egg and then the vanilla.

Using a fork or balloon whisk, whisk the cocoa, both flours, bicarbonate of soda and salt together in a bowl. Add to the butter mixture in 3 or 4 additions, beating after each, but only just enough to incorporate the flour—overbeating could make the cookies tough.

Roll tablespoons of the mixture into balls, about 15g/½oz each, and arrange on the prepared baking sheet with a 5-cm/2-in gap between them. Flatten with your palm to make discs 3cm/1¼in in diameter.

Bake for about 8 minutes. The cookies will be soft but will firm up as they cool. Leave on the baking sheet for 5 minutes, then transfer to a wire rack to cool completely. Repeat with the rest of the mixture.

While the cookies are cooling, beat all the filling ingredients together in a bowl or stand mixer until creamy and smooth, adding salt to taste (this will depend on the saltiness of the peanut butter you use). Chill until needed.

When the cookies are completely cool, spread some of the filling over the smooth side of one cookie, then sandwich another one on top. Repeat with the rest of the filling and cookies.

Chocolate and cheese: a match made in heaven or hell? British chocolatier and flavour genius Paul A. Young adores the pairing if the balance of flavours is right. In his cookbook *Adventures with Chocolate*, he marries bacon, Stilton and chocolate in a toasted sandwich (the salt/sweet/fat combination is joyous, if you've never tried it) and enthuses about the union of goat's cheese and lemon ganache in dark chocolates. Although the combination of ingredients might seem odd, it actually works because they share some of the same flavour notes: chocolate can carry hints of cheese, along with other types of dairy such as yogurt and cream.

In this recipe, the pairing is much less dramatic, with just a hint of cocoa from the nibs, which works wonderfully with all kinds of cheese.

MAKES ABOUT 20 CRACKERS

70g/2½oz plain [all-purpose] flour, plus extra for dusting
70g 2½oz spelt flour
½ tsp fine sea salt
30g/1oz glacé [candied] cherries, chopped small but not fine
25g/1oz dried cranberries, chopped small but not fine
20g/¾oz pistachios, chopped small but not fine
20g/¾oz cacao nibs
about 60ml/2fl oz milk
1 Tbsp honey
1 Tbsp olive oil

Preheat the oven to 170°C/340°F/Gas mark 3 and line a large baking sheet with baking paper.

Using a fork or balloon whisk, whisk both flours and the salt together in a mixing bowl to combine. Add the cherries, cranberries, pistachios and nibs and stir well to evenly distribute them, breaking up any that have clumped together. Stir in the milk, honey and olive oil.

Knead the dough briefly on a lightly floured work surface and shape into a ball. Lightly dust all over with flour, and place in the centre of a sheet of baking paper. Place another sheet of baking paper on top, flatten the dough a little with your hand, then roll out evenly to a thickness of 3mm/⅛in, or until large enough to stamp out 20 × 6-cm/2½-in round crackers. Carefully peel off the top sheet of baking paper.

Using a 6-cm/2½-in cutter dipped in flour (I use a wine glass), stamp out circles of dough and transfer to the prepared baking sheet. Knead the dough scraps together, re-roll and continue stamping out circles until all the dough is used up. (Depending on the size of your baking sheet, you might have to bake the crackers in batches. I find the results are more consistent this way than baking them on 2 sheets on different shelves in the oven.)

Bake for 12–15 minutes, flipping the crackers over roughly halfway through so they colour evenly on both sides. As with all crackers, cookies and biscuits, you need to watch these like a hawk as they will burn easily. I prefer them quite pale, which means they're still a little soft, even when cool. But if you let them bake until pale gold they crisp up nicely. Transfer to a wire rack to cool completely before serving.

BEEF AND CHOCOLATE PIES ('MPANATIGGHI)

If you find yourself in a certain alleyway in Modica, Sicily (and I highly recommend that you arrange for this to happen) your nose will take you where you need to go: Antica Dolceria Bonajuto. There are many chocolate makers in this opulent Baroque town, but this one is an institution. Founded in 1880, the wood-panelled shop still produces award-winning cinnamon, vanilla and chilli chocolate made in the style of the Aztecs — without conching, tempering or adding extra fat. Because the temperature of the chocolate never exceeds 45°C/113°F, the sugar never completely melts, resulting in a crunchy, highly textured bar that's distinctive to Modica. The Spanish, who once ruled Sicily, introduced the technique after discovering it in the New World — and Modica is one of the few places outside Latin America where chocolate is still made in this style.

Among Antica Dolceria Bonajuto's range of chocolate treats you will also find *'mpanatigghi*, little empanada-style pies stuffed with minced [ground] beef, Modica chocolate, spices and almonds. Legend has it these extraordinary morsels were invented in the 1600s by nuns of the Origlione monastery in Palermo, as a surreptitious way to partake of meat during Lent, when it was forbidden. Another theory suggests making the pies was a way to preserve meat in times of abundance. What is certain is that there's nothing meaty at all about them, and that they're heavenly eaten warm from the oven. In Modica, recipes for *'mpanatigghi* are closely guarded, but Pierpaolo Ruta — the sixth generation of his family to run the business — very kindly shared his recipe with me. This is my adapted version.

MAKES 16

FOR THE PASTRY

350g/12oz plain [all-purpose] flour,
  plus extra for dusting
90g/3¼oz icing [confectioners'] sugar,
  plus extra, sifted for dusting
100g/3½oz cold lard or butter
4 large egg yolks, lightly beaten
100ml/3½fl oz cold water

FOR THE FILLING

65g/2¼oz good-quality lean beef
  (not ready-bought mince/ground
  beef), finely chopped
70g/2½oz ground almonds
75g/2¾oz caster [superfine] sugar
10g/⅓oz cocoa powder
25g/1oz dark chocolate (about
  70% cocoa solids), grated
1 tsp ground cinnamon
2 large egg whites

Start with the pastry. Using a fork or balloon whisk, whisk the flour and sugar together in a bowl to combine. Grate in the lard or butter and rub it in with your fingertips until you have small pieces of fat—maybe slightly larger than grains of rice—coated in flour. Stir in the egg yolks, then add the cold water, a little at a time, stirring to bring the mixture together into a scraggy dough. Knead lightly in the bowl until smooth, then shape into a disc, wrap in plastic wrap and chill for at least 1 hour.

Now, make the filling. Fry the beef in a dry frying pan, moving the meat around constantly, until browned. Set aside to cool for 5 minutes. Place the remaining ingredients in a food processor, add the cool meat and blitz to a paste. Scrape into a small bowl and chill until needed.

When you're ready to make the pies, preheat the oven to 180°C/350°F/Gas mark 4 and line 1 large or 2 small baking sheets with baking paper. Roll out the dough on a lightly dusted work surface to 3mm/⅛in thick. Using a 10-cm/4-in cutter or small bowl, cut out 16 rounds and transfer to the prepared baking sheet as you go.

Place 1 level tablespoon of the filling in the centre of each pastry circle. Lightly brush the edges with water and fold the pastry over the filling; gently press around the filling with your thumbs to remove any air pockets, and lightly press the pastry layers together to seal.

Trim the pies using a cutter roughly 7cm/2¾in in diameter—I use a fluted cookie cutter, but you could use a glass dipped in flour. Place the cutter over the half-moon-shaped pies so that the filling is roughly in the centre. Press down to cut away excess pastry, making sure not to cut into the filling, and to leave a sealed edge all the way around. Using scissors, snip the top of each pastry to make a small air hole.

Bake for 15 minutes, or until the bottoms of the pies are pale gold. The tops will be firm but not brown. Leave to cool a little and dust with icing sugar before serving.

FLAPJACKS WITH PINEAPPLE CHOCOLATE GANACHE

Flapjacks, the quintessentially English traybake (not to be confused with the pancake version of the same name enjoyed in the US), are often misrepresented as health food, presumably because there are oats in the mix. Who is anyone kidding? The truth is, flapjacks are a joyful extravagance of sugar, syrup and butter. There are those who might argue, therefore, that adding chocolate isn't necessary, but I'm not in that camp. The pineapple ganache on top is utterly delicious, and simply adds extra decadence to proceedings. I sometimes use a fruity 72% Madagascan chocolate from Pump Street Bakery for the ganache, which works a treat, or Venezuelan with notes of tropical fruit.

MAKES 16 FLAPJACKS
145g/5oz unsalted butter
3 Tbsp golden [corn] syrup
150g/5¼oz porridge oats
150g/5¼oz spelt flour
60g/2¼oz soft dark brown sugar
1½ tsp ground cinnamon
good pinch of salt

150g/5¼oz chopped dried pineapple
 (or other dried tropical fruit)

FOR THE GANACHE
165g/5¾oz dark chocolate (around 70%
 cocoa solids), grated or finely chopped
150ml/5fl oz pure pineapple juice

Preheat the oven to 180°C/350°F/Gas mark 4. Line the base and sides of a 20 × 20-cm/8 × 8-in brownie tray or baking dish with baking paper, cutting slits in each corner so it fits neatly. Let the paper hang over the edges so you can use it as handles to lift the cooked flapjack out of the tray.

In a small pan, melt the butter and syrup together, then set aside.

Using a fork or balloon whisk, whisk the oats, flour, sugar, cinnamon and salt together in a bowl, then stir in the pineapple.

Pour the melted butter into the flour and oats mixture and stir thoroughly to combine, making sure all the dry ingredients, especially the bits at the bottom of the bowl, are soaked in butter.

Tip the mixture into the prepared brownie tray and press in firmly and evenly with your hands — you need to use some pressure so there are no gaps, otherwise the flapjacks will crumble.

Bake for 20 minutes if you prefer your flapjacks slightly soft or 25 minutes if you prefer them crispier — either way, they'll still be chewy. Leave to cool in the tray.

When the flapjacks are completely cool, make the ganache—don't do it ahead of time, as the chocolate will set, and you'll have to re-melt it. Place the chocolate in a heatproof bowl. Pour the pineapple juice into a small pan and simmer until reduced to 100ml/3½fl oz—I keep a small heatproof measuring jug next to the hob [stove] and pour the juice back and forth until sufficiently reduced. Immediately pour the hot juice over the chocolate and stir until completely melted. (If a few bits of chocolate stubbornly refuse to melt, sit the bowl over a pan of barely simmering water and stir.)

Pour the chocolate over the flapjack and spread to cover completely. Set aside for 1 hour or so until set, then lift out of the brownie tray and cut into squares with a sharp knife.

AFTER EIGHT BROWNIES

The Proust effect of After Eights—or After Dinner Mints, as they are called in Australia—is profound. Just the sight of one of those sleek black pockets drags me back to the 1970s when I was a kid and getting up in the morning to discover the wreckage of the previous night's parental dinner party. Amid the half empty wine bottles and dirty glasses, would be a slew of discarded After Eight pockets. I would search through every single one, inhaling the minty-ness as I went, just in case a chocolate had—mysteriously, joyously—been overlooked. Invariably, one had. This is my homage to those gorgeous squares of chocolate-coated mint fondant.

MAKES 16 SQUARES

230g/8oz unsalted butter, softened, plus extra for greasing
100g/3½oz plain [all-purpose] flour
85g/3oz cocoa powder
2 tsp instant coffee granules
½ tsp fine sea salt
½ tsp baking powder

about 280g/10oz After Eight mints (28 mints)
300g/10½oz caster [superfine] sugar
3 large eggs, lightly beaten
1 tsp vanilla extract
10g/⅓oz fresh mint leaves, finely chopped

Preheat the oven to 180°C/350°F/Gas mark 4. Butter a 20 × 20-cm/8 × 8-in brownie or baking tray and line with baking paper, making slits in the corners so it fits neatly. Let the paper overhang the sides so you can lift the cooked brownie out.

Using a fork or balloon whisk, whisk the flour, cocoa powder, coffee granules, salt and baking powder together in a bowl and set aside.

Set aside 16 of the After Eights and roughly chop the rest.

Beat the butter and sugar together in a stand mixer or in a bowl with electric beaters until fluffy. Gradually beat in the eggs and vanilla. Stir in the flour mixture until just combined, then fold in the chopped After Eights and the mint leaves.

Scrape the batter into the prepared tray, making sure to fill the corners, and smooth the top. Arrange the remaining After Eights neatly on top and press them down just a little into the batter.

Bake for about 25–30 minutes: the top will be very soft from the melted After Eights, but the centre should be just set and not wobbly. Leave in the tin to cool completely, then lift out and cut into squares. A hot knife makes this easy: just run under hot water and dry between slices.

PASSIONFRUIT AND ORANGE CURD TARTLETS
WITH SUMAC AND CHOCOLATE

Sometimes unlikely chocolate pairings work extremely well, and thus it is with sumac, a pretty purple spice grown in the Middle East and the Mediterranean. Actually, it's not surprising that the combination works, as ground sumac has a tangy lemon flavour and chocolate pairs beautifully with citrus. There's only a little used here, but it really adds a tangy hint of fruitiness to the chocolate. You will need 6 × 10-cm/4-in loose-bottomed tartlet tins.

MAKES 6 LITTLE TARTLETS

FOR THE CURD

10 large passionfruit, yielding about
   165g/5¾oz pulp
finely grated zest of 1 large orange
100g/3½oz unsalted butter, melted
   and cooled a little
100g/3½oz caster [superfine] sugar
2 large eggs plus 2 egg yolks,
   lightly beaten

FOR THE PASTRY

195g/7oz plain [all-purpose] flour,
   plus extra for dusting
120g/4¼oz unsalted very cold
   butter, chopped
30g/1oz caster [superfine] sugar
1 tsp white wine vinegar
¼ tsp fine sea salt
about 50ml/1⅔fl oz cold water

FOR THE CHOCOLATE

180g/6oz dark chocolate (60% cocoa
   solids), chopped
1½ tsp sumac

Start with the curd. Scoop the passionfruit pulp into a small pan and gently warm through. Don't let it boil; a little heat just makes it easier to separate out the seeds. Push the pulp through a sieve [strainer] set over a heatproof bowl (one that will sit over a pan) using the back of a spoon. Remember to scrape the pulp from the underside of the sieve until all you have left are seeds. Add the remaining curd ingredients to the bowl and stir to combine.

Set the bowl over a pan of barely simmering water and stir constantly—I stir with a whisk—until the mixture thickens to a custard consistency. This will take around 10 minutes. Transfer to a bowl, cover with plastic wrap so that it touches the curd to prevent a skin forming and leave to cool completely, or chill overnight for the best results.

To make the pastry, place all the ingredients, except the water, in a food processor and pulse to a breadcrumb consistency. Add the water gradually, until the mixture comes together into a ball. Turn out onto a lightly floured work surface, knead briefly, then shape into a disc and chill for at least 2 hours. Get your 6 × 10-cm/ 4-in loose-bottomed tartlet tins ready.

Roll out the pastry on a lightly floured work surface to 3mm/⅛in thick. Cut out 14-cm/5½-in circles using a plate or bowl as a guide. Place a pastry circle centrally over one of the tartlet tins and gently press it in with your fingers. Use an offcut of pastry rolled into a ball and dipped in flour to gently push the pastry into the fluted sides of the tin, and into the edge where the sides meet the base. You should have an overhang of pastry all around, so gently push the excess back into the tin to reinforce the edge — this will allow for shrinkage in the oven. Repeat with the rest of the dough and tins, then chill for 20 minutes.

Meanwhile, preheat the oven to 170°C/340°F/Gas mark 3.

When the pastry cases have chilled, line them with a double layer of foil and fill with baking beans or rice. Bake for 20 minutes, then remove the foil and beans and bake for a further 5–10 minutes until pale gold. Leave to cool completely in their tins.

Melt the chocolate in a heatproof bowl set over a pan of barely simmering water, making sure the bottom of the bowl doesn't touch the water. Stir in the sumac. Spoon about 25g/1oz of the chocolate into each cooled pastry case, spread over the base and leave to set. Stir the passionfruit curd to loosen and spoon over the set chocolate — you want to fill the tart cases to the top. Serve immediately.

TOASTED ALMOND, AMARETTO AND MILK CHOCOLATE BLONDIES

There's a theory that blondies might well have been the original brownies. The *Boston Cooking-School Cookbook* by Fannie Merritt Farmer, published in 1896, contained what's believed to be the first ever recipe to be called 'brownies' — except they didn't contain any chocolate. Instead, their dark colour came from molasses. Farmer later updated her recipe, renaming them 'blonde brownies', suggesting that by this time a similar baked goody was being made with chocolate.

Their past might be inscrutable, but fudgy and butterscotchy blondies are just as delicious as their chocolate-filled twins.

MAKES 16 × 5-CM / 2-IN SQUARES
180g/6oz unsalted butter
60g/2¼oz blanched almonds
250g/8¾oz plain [all-purpose] flour
½ tsp baking powder
½ tsp fine sea salt
280g/10oz soft dark brown sugar

2 large eggs, lightly beaten
60ml/2fl oz amaretto (rum also
   works well)
200g/7oz milk chocolate, chopped (or
   use a mix of milk and white chocolate
   if you like), roughly chopped

Preheat the oven to 170°C/340°F/Gas mark 3. Line the base and sides of a 20 × 20-cm/8 × 8-in brownie tray or baking dish with baking paper, cutting slits in each corner so it fits neatly. Let the paper hang over the edges so you can lift the cooked blondie out of the tray.

Melt the butter in a small pan and set aside to cool. Meanwhile, spread the almonds out on a baking sheet and roast for 6–8 minutes until golden brown — watch them carefully as they burn easily. When done, roughly chop and set aside.

Using a fork or balloon whisk, whisk the flour, baking powder and salt together in a bowl and set aside.

Add the sugar to the melted butter and stir to combine. Stir in the eggs and then the amaretto.

Fold the sugary butter mixture into the flour; don't overmix or the blondies will be tough. Fold in the almonds and chocolate. Pour the batter into the prepared tray, making sure to fill the corners, and smooth the top. Bake for 25 minutes, or until firm on top, just about cooked on the inside and a skewer inserted into the centre comes out with some chocolate and crumbs. You want the blondies to be fudgy in the middle. Leave to cool in the tray for 10 minutes, then lift out and cool on a wire rack before cutting into squares.

PISTACHIO, CITRUS AND DARK CHOCOLATE CINNAMON ROLLS

Like the Black Sesame Seed and Dark Chocolate Brioche Loaf on page 106, these rolls make a decadent brunch, served warm from the oven, with a pot of good strong coffee on the side.

MAKES 7 ROLLS

FOR THE DOUGH

240ml/8fl oz whole milk

50g/1¾oz unsalted butter, cut into
   pieces, plus extra for greasing

400g/14oz strong white bread flour,
   plus extra for dusting

7g/¼oz fast-action dried [active
   dry] yeast

¾ tsp fine sea salt

1 large egg, lightly beaten

flavourless vegetable oil, for oiling

1 egg yolk, lightly beaten, for brushing

FOR THE FILLING

80g/2¾oz pistachios, finely chopped

115g/4oz soft dark brown sugar

1 tsp ground cinnamon

80g/2¾oz dark chocolate (between
   70–80% cocoa solids), chopped

50g/1¾oz mixed citrus peel

80g/2¾oz unsalted butter, soft

To make the dough, heat the milk in a small pan until almost boiling. Remove the pan from the heat, add the butter and stir until melted. Set aside to cool to lukewarm.

Meanwhile, in a mixing bowl or the bowl of a stand mixer, whisk the flour, yeast and salt together. Add the whole beaten egg and then the cooled milk. Knead with a dough hook attachment for 5 minutes or turn out onto a lightly floured work surface and knead by hand for 8–10 minutes. The dough will be quite sticky at first but becomes smooth and elastic as you knead — add a little more flour if it's too wet to work with.

Place the dough in a large lightly oiled bowl (it will expand considerably) and turn over to coat. Cover with a clean tea [dish] towel and set aside somewhere warm for 1 hour, or until doubled in size.

While you're waiting, mix all the filling ingredients, except the butter, together. Butter a 23-cm/9-in round loose-bottomed or springform cake tin with sides at least 5cm/2in high. Wrap the base in foil, as the filling sometimes melts and seeps out a little.

When the dough has risen, press down on it to let the air out and tip out onto a lightly floured work surface. Roll into a rectangle roughly 35 × 25cm/14 × 10in, making sure the middle is no thicker than the edges. With the long side of the dough parallel to the edge of your work surface, spread the butter evenly over the top. Sprinkle over the filling and press down on it gently. Working with the long side, carefully roll the dough into a sausage shape, like a Swiss [jelly] roll.

Cut into 7 equal pieces each about 5cm/2in long and arrange, cut-side up, in the prepared tin: place one roll in the centre and the others around it, with a little space in between. Cover with a clean tea towel and set aside for 30 minutes. Preheat the oven to 180°C/350°F/Gas mark 4.

Brush the tops of the rolls with the beaten egg yolk and bake for 20–25 minutes until golden on top. Leave in the tin for 5 minutes, then release and pull apart when cool enough to handle. These are delicious served warm but will keep well in an airtight container for a couple of days.

CHERRY, COCONUT AND CHOCOLATE SLICE

Cherry Ripe poses a confectionery conundrum. It's a widely adored and iconic chocolate bar devoured by millions in Australia, but inexplicably (and frustratingly) very hard to find beyond those shores. Being born and raised in Australia, I've been addicted to the insanely tasty combination of dark chocolate, chopped glacé [candied] cherries and coconut for years. As I no longer live in Australia, this lovely slice keeps me happy between care parcels from home.

MAKES 10 SLICES

FOR THE BASE
180g/6oz unsalted butter, softened
90g/3¼oz icing [confectioners'] sugar
170g/6oz plain [all-purpose] flour
4½ Tbsp cocoa powder
½ tsp fine sea salt

FOR THE TOPPING
450g/15¾oz glacé [candied] cherries
135g/4¾oz condensed milk
170g/6oz desiccated [shredded] coconut
70g/2½oz dried cherries, roughly
 chopped
35g/1¼oz cacao nibs

Line the base and sides of a 20 × 20-cm/8 × 8-in brownie tray or baking dish with baking paper, cutting slits in each corner so it fits neatly. Let the paper hang over the edges so you can use it as handles to lift the cooked slices out of the tray.

Start with the base. Beat the butter in a stand mixer or in a bowl with electric beaters until creamy, then gradually beat in the icing sugar until light and fluffy. Add the flour, cocoa powder and salt, and beat on low speed — or stir by hand — until the flour is well combined and the mixture smooth. Don't overbeat or the base will be tough. Scrape the mixture into the prepared tray, spread out evenly and chill for 30 minutes. Preheat the oven to 160°C/325°F/Gas mark 3.

Bake the base for 15–20 minutes until firm to touch. Leave to cool but leave the oven on.

Meanwhile, make the topping. Blitz the glacé cherries to a paste in a food processor. Transfer to a bowl, add the remaining topping ingredients and mix until well combined.

Spread the topping evenly over the base and smooth the top with the back of a spoon. Bake for 25 minutes, or until golden and bubbling — the topping will still be quite soft but will firm up as it cools. Leave to cool completely in the tray, then lift out and cut into squares.

CHOCOLATE BRIOCHE DOUGHNUTS WITH
BAY CARAMEL CUSTARD AND NIB SUGAR

Making these beauties is a project, without question, but they require far less effort than you might think. The most time-consuming part is waiting for the dough to rise and prove, so you can mostly go about your business, but with a little skip in your step at the prospect of truly lovely doughnuts. I had a great time experimenting with different fillings and glazes—delicious, but as is the way with doughnuts, teeth-achingly sweet. These are less so, tempered by the subtle savoury flavour of bay, which partners beautifully with caramel and chocolate. The nib sugar recipe is from the truly fantastic book *Making Chocolate: From Bean to Bar to S'more* by the team behind Dandelion Chocolate in the US.

MAKES 12 DOUGHNUTS

FOR THE CHOCOLATE BRIOCHE
220g/7¾oz strong white bread flour
30g/1oz cocoa powder
30g/1oz caster [superfine] sugar
7g/¼oz fast-action dried [active
  dry] yeast
¼ tsp fine sea salt
3 large eggs, lightly beaten
125g/4½oz unsalted butter, at room
  temperature (but not too soft),
  cut into pieces
flavourless vegetable oil, for oiling
about 1.5 litres/50fl oz vegetable
  oil, such as sunflower or rapeseed
  [canola], for deep-frying

FOR THE BAY CARAMEL
3 medium-large dried bay leaves
70g/2½oz caster [superfine] sugar
35g/1¼oz unsalted butter
50ml/1⅔fl oz double [heavy] cream
2 Tbsp water
generous pinch of sea salt flakes

FOR THE CUSTARD
80ml/2¾fl oz whole milk
45ml/1½fl oz double [heavy] cream
2 egg yolks
25g/1oz caster [superfine] sugar
15g/½oz cornflour [cornstarch]

FOR THE NIB SUGAR
10g/⅓oz cacao nibs
65g/1¼oz caster [superfine] sugar
1 heaped tsp ground cinnamon
pinch of fine sea salt

First, make the brioche. Place the flour, cocoa, sugar, yeast and salt in a stand mixer and stir to combine. Add the eggs. Using the dough hook attachment, mix on low speed for 5 minutes, stopping to scrape down the bowl a couple of times, until all the flour is incorporated. Increase the speed to medium and mix for 10 minutes.

Reduce the speed to low and add the butter, a few pieces at a time. When the butter is used up, increase the speed to medium and mix for a further 10 minutes, or until the dough is shiny, elastic and comes away from the sides of the bowl cleanly.

Tip out onto a work surface and press out to form a rectangle about 1cm/⅜in thick. Fold one-third of the dough over onto itself, then do the same with the other side. Repeat with the top and the bottom. Place the dough, seam-side down, in a large oiled bowl—the dough needs space to expand—cover with oiled plastic wrap and set aside somewhere warm for an hour or so until doubled in size.

Meanwhile, line a large baking sheet with baking paper. When the dough has risen, press your hand into it to release some air and break off about twelve 45-g/1½-oz pieces, about the size of a large golf ball. Gently flatten on your work surface, then bring the edges together into the middle, holding them in place with your thumb. Turn the dough over so the join is at the bottom. Cup your hand over the dough and using firm pressure roll on the work surface to make a smooth tight ball. Transfer to the prepared baking sheet and repeat with the rest of the dough, leaving a 3-cm/1¼-in space between each ball. Cover with oiled plastic wrap and set aside for about 1 hour, or until increased in size by 50 per cent. (The time this takes depends on how warm your kitchen is).

While this is happening, make the bay caramel custard. Place the bay leaves and a few spoonfuls of the sugar in a spice or coffee grinder and blitz to a powder. Mix with the rest of the sugar.

Have the butter and cream ready by the hob [stove]. Place the sugar and water in a small pan, stir to combine and set over a medium heat. Bring to a simmer, swirling the pan now and then (don't stir) until the sugar has dissolved. Simmer until the mixture turns a deep amber colour. Remove from the heat and stir in the cream—beware, as it will splatter—and then stir in the butter and salt. Set the caramel aside.

For the custard, place the milk and cream in a small pan. Bring almost to the boil then remove from the heat. In a bowl, stir the egg yolks, sugar, cornflour and just enough of the hot milk mixture together to make a very loose paste. Gradually stir in the rest of the milk, then transfer the lot back into the pan. Cook over a gentle heat, stirring constantly, until thickened. Don't let it boil. Remove from the heat and stir in the caramel, then return the pan to a gentle heat, stirring, until thick. Don't let the mixture get too hot or it will separate and use a whisk if needed to remove any lumps. Transfer to a disposable piping bag, fasten closed with a clip and leave to cool completely.

To make the nib sugar, finely grind the nibs to a powder in a spice or coffee grinder. Combine with the sugar, cinnamon and salt and place in a shallow bowl.

To fry the doughnuts, place enough oil in a large heavy pan (a cast-iron casserole [Dutch oven] is perfect) to come 5cm/2in up the sides and heat to between 170–180°C/340–350°F. Have a wire rack lined with paper towels by the side of the hob.

Lower 2 or 3 doughnuts at a time into the hot oil. Fry for about 1 minute on each side until puffed up and golden. It's important to keep adjusting the temperature —or even remove the pan from the heat—now and then, to ensure the oil doesn't get too hot or cool. Remove the cooked doughnuts with a slotted spoon to the wire rack.

While the doughnuts are still warm, cut a slit in the side of each and pipe in a generous amount of the caramel custard, then roll in the nib sugar. They are best eaten warm.

"...When he could stand it no longer, he would peel back a tiny bit of the paper wrapping at one corner to expose a tiny bit of chocolate, and then he would take a tiny nibble — just enough to allow the lovely sweet taste to spread out slowly over his tongue. The next day, he would take another tiny nibble, and so on, and so on. And in this way, Charlie would make his sixpenny bar of birthday chocolate last him for more than a month." — Roald Dahl, *Charlie and the Chocolate Factory*

This quote from the first chapter of Dahl's children's classic hurt my 10-year-old heart every time I devoured the words. It's where Dahl introduces the hero of the tale, Charlie Bucket, and explains that his family is so desperately poor they can only afford to buy him chocolate once a year for his birthday. Charlie always looks at the bar for a long time before tasting it, not quite believing it really is his. Then he limits himself to a tiny morsel each day to stretch out the joy. How badly I felt for Charlie.

First published in the US in 1964, Dahl's depiction of the poor chocolate-obsessed boy and the magical factory where his favourite treat flows in a river, tapped into the world's fascination with chocolate, and the particular delight it brought to children, including me. The novel also highlights how perfectly chocolate lends itself to fiction; novels are awash with the stuff, luring us in with a tantalizing blend of narrative and deliciousness. A whole genre of romantic 'choc lit' exists for readers with a taste for love stories laced with cocoa, and similarly, a rich seam of crime fiction also has chocolate at the centre of the mystery. Readers not only covet what the characters are eating, but chocolate triggers an emotional response, often nostalgia, sometimes joy and occasionally sadness. Chocolate can symbolize sensuality, indulgence or a sense of the exotic. It can imbue a book with enchantment or mystery. Chocolate speaks all languages (in the developed world at least) and knows no boundaries. It's the perfect vehicle for authors to convey their fictional visions.

Charlie and the Chocolate Factory tugged at the heartstrings of adolescent me, but more than that, it carried me off on a fantastic journey that aligns with chocolate's exotic, mystical origins. While the ancient civilizations believed cacao was a gift from the underworld, Willy Wonka, the eccentric confectionery inventor at the centre of the story, conjures chocolate in a fantastical sugary landscape of minty meadows and flavourful flowers where everything is edible. A river made entirely from hot melted chocolate flows through this rural idyll, and is frothed, not as the Mayans did by pouring it from one vessel to another, but in a waterfall.

In Dahl's vision, doll-sized humans called Oompa Loompas work in the factory, and here chocolate mirrors the real world, as it sometimes does in fiction. Dahl rewrote this section after facing accusations of racism. In the first edition—which appeared in US bookshops the same year President Lyndon Johnson signed the Civil Rights Act with Martin Luther King standing beside him— the Oompa Loompas were explicitly described as black pygmies from Africa whom Wonka, the fearless imperial explorer, had imported to the factory. Their skin was almost black, Dahl told readers, and Charlie even asked if they were made of chocolate. According to Lucy Mangan in her book *Inside Charlie's Chocolate Factory,* Dahl insisted there was never any racial intent in his depiction. He willingly deleted references to blackness and Africa in later editions, rewriting the Oompa Loompas to have 'rosy white skin' and hailing from an invented Loompaland.

I also adore J.K. Rowling's use of chocolate as a mystical symbol in the Harry Potter series, and she evokes its legendary status as a balm for unhappiness. In her wizard world, chocolate serves as an antidote to the effects of the evil Dementors, fearsome creatures that feed off human happiness and trigger despair in their victims. In *The Prisoner of Azkaban* (1999), Harry and his friends encounter a Dementor on the Hogwarts Express and their new teacher, Professor Lupin, dispenses treatment in the form of chocolate.

"A loud snap made them all jump. Professor Lupin was breaking an enormous slab of chocolate into pieces. 'Here,' he said to Harry, handing him a particularly large piece. 'Eat it. It'll help.'"

Honeydukes, Rowling's supernatural sweet shop, sells 'hundreds of different kinds of chocolate in neat rows'. Among them are Chocolate Cauldrons filled with Firewhiskey, which Romilda Vane spikes with love potion and gives to Harry in *Harry Potter and the Half-Blood Prince* (2005), echoing centuries-old tales of chocolate being used as a vehicle for poison. Most famous of all are the chocolate frogs Harry and Ron encounter on the Hogwarts Express; they are made from the magical substance Croakoa, which presumably gives them the power to hop like the real thing.

But chocolate enchantment is not confined to children's fiction. Colombian novelist Gabriel García Márquez features chocolate in his magical realism saga, *One Hundred Years of Solitude* (1967). Father Nicanor Reyna is so disturbed by the lack of religious faith in Macondo, the isolated town where the tale is set, and hoping to raise money to build a church, tries to convince its heathen citizens that God exists by levitating 15cm off the ground, fuelled by hot chocolate.

"He went among the houses for several days repeating the demonstration of levitation by means of chocolate, while the acolyte collected so much money in a bag that in less than a month he began the construction of the church. No one doubted the divine origin of the demonstration..."

Márquez ingeniously intertwines the concept of holy wine and the divine nature of chocolate to create a unique magic drink that allows a priest to fly. Chocolate was associated with blood and sacrifice in ancient Mesoamerica, while wine represents the blood of Christ in Christian theology. By bringing the Old and New Worlds together, chocolate's special power enables Father Nicanor to perform a miracle.

In her bestselling novel *Chocolat* (1991), Joanne Harris evokes a different kind of magic in her sensuous tale about Vianne Rocher, who arrives in a tiny French village with her young daughter to set up a chocolate shop. Grumpy villagers fall under the spell of the charming chocolatier, who can mysteriously anticipate their favourite treats without them saying a word. Over a mug of hot chocolate or a bite of a luscious bonbon, they succumb to the pleasure of simple things; in the process they reveal to Vianne their secrets and rediscover joy in their lives.

Vianne says, "I sell dreams, small comforts, sweet harmless temptations to bring down a multitude of saints crash-crash-crashing among the hazels and nougatines. Is that so bad?"

Of course, the priest of the parish, Francis Reynaud, equates pleasure with sin and is convinced that Vianne is a witch set on luring his upstanding flock into over-indulgence. This thread of the story mirrors ancient associations between women, witchcraft and chocolate, and the trope that cocoa is delicious — but also somehow bad. In the modernist masterpiece *Ulysses* (1922), James Joyce goes further, linking chocolate to licentiousness and prostitution. In the fifteenth episode, 'Circe', Leopold Bloom finds himself in a brothel in Dublin's red light district, and offers chocolate to the prostitute Zoe Higgins. "Fingers was made before forks," she says, tearing open the silver foil. Unbridled sexuality proceeds to turn everyone into literal animals.

Most infamous of all for linking chocolate and sex in fiction is Donatien Alphonse François, aka the Marquis de Sade (1740–1814). The French nobleman, politician and author of pornographic novels was also a gourmand and chocolate lover. Rumoured to have served aphrodisiac-laced chocolates to guests in real life, he also featured chocolate in his fiction, furthering its (essentially baseless) reputation as an aphrodisiac. In his steamy *The 120 Days of Sodom* (1904) he wrote:

"At eleven o'clock they passed into the women's quarters where the eight young sultanas appeared naked, and in this state served chocolate."

More tamely but utterly beautifully and poignantly, chocolate and passion pulse through Mexican author Laura Esquivel's *Like Water For Chocolate* (1989), a masterful feast of a novel in which food is infused with the emotion of the cook, and then passed on to those who eat it. Tita, the protagonist, is destined for a life as a single woman thanks to Mexican tradition that demands the youngest daughter stay at home to look after the mother until she dies. But Tita falls in love with Pedro who, in desperation, marries her sister Rosaura so he can be near his true love. Tita is consumed with anger and, I assume, sexual frustration.

"Tita was literally 'like water for chocolate' [hot chocolate is made with water rather than milk in Mexico] — she was on the verge of boiling over."

But in Esquivel's vision, chocolate also symbolizes nurturing and the reassuring comfort of home. Tita cherishes memories of her childhood when Nacha, the cook who fed and raised her, whipped hot chocolate in the kitchen. And Tita's sister Gertrudis, returning home after a long absence, says she has come back for a cup of freshly whipped chocolate.

"Gertrudis closed her eyes each time she took a sip from the cup of chocolate she had in front of her. Life would be much nicer if one could carry the smells and tastes of the maternal home wherever one pleased."

This theme of home and families being brought together by chocolate is common in many of my favourite books. English children's author Enid Blyton clearly adored chocolate, liberally including it in her vivid descriptions of farmhouse teas and picnics. Chocolate cakes, biscuits and blancmange, along with boxes and bars of the stuff, are all on the menu, sustaining the children during their adventures. They devour chocolate throughout *The Faraway Tree* series of novels (1939–51), for example, as they encounter goblins, pixies and fairies in the enchanted wood. Echoing messages contained in chocolate advertising of the period, Blyton's mothers regard chocolate almost as an essential part of a nourishing, wholesome diet.

"The children ate their breakfast quickly. Mother told Bessie and Fanny to cut sandwiches for themselves and to take a small chocolate cake from the larder. 'You can take a packet of biscuits, too,' she said, 'and there are apples in that dish over there. If you are hungry when you come home to-night I will bake you some potatoes in the oven, and you can eat them in their skins with salt and butter.'"

Likewise, in the novel *Little Women* (1868, 1869), Louisa May Alcott focuses on the importance of home and family as she tells the story of the March sisters, Meg, Jo, Beth and Amy, who live in genteel poverty in small town America. Alcott employs chocolate and other luxury foods to teach Amy a lesson in virtue and the importance of staying true to oneself. When Amy wants to impress a group of rich friends from her drawing class by inviting them home for a lavish lunch, her mother suggests a modest spread would be more appropriate. But Amy demurs.

"Oh dear, no! We must have cold tongue and chicken, French chocolate and ice cream, besides. The girls are used to such things, and I want my lunch to be proper and elegant, though I do work for my living."

Needless to say, the event is a disaster: "...the chicken too tough, the tongue too salt and the chocolate wouldn't froth properly." Amy learns a painful lesson.

Chocolate has long been a literary cipher for overindulgence and excess, harking back to the centuries when it was such an exotic and outrageously expensive item that only the uber-rich could afford it. In *A Tale of Two Cities* (1859), Charles Dickens wields chocolate as a savage literary device to mock the extravagance and indolence of the upper classes. Monseigneur, a greedy self-important French aristocrat (a symbol of the aristocracy generally), requires no fewer than four flunkeys to serve him his breakfast chocolate.

"One lacquey carried the chocolate-pot into the sacred presence; a second, milled and frothed the chocolate with the instrument he bore for that function; a third, presented the favoured napkin; a fourth (of the two gold watches), poured the chocolate out. It was impossible for Monseigneur to dispense with one of these attendants on the chocolate and hold his high place under the admiring Heavens. Deep would have been the blot upon his escutcheon if his chocolate had been ignobly waited on by only three men; he must have died of two."

To drive home his disgust at the yawning inequality between the classes, Dickens juxtaposes this scene with another where a large cask of wine is dropped in the street, and the contents pool between the cobblestones. The poor and destitute rush to scoop it up with their hands "or even with handkerchiefs from women's heads, which were squeezed dry into infants' mouths."

But chocolate often brings redemption and joy in books, too. Happily for Charlie Bucket, chocolate delivers financial salvation to his family eventually; as the 'least rotten child' he inherits the chocolate factory and forevermore can enjoy as much of his favourite treat as he likes.

I leave the final word to the late US author, journalist and film-maker Nora Ephron, whose deliciously warm and witty auto-biographical novel, *Heartburn* (1983) is one of my very favourite books. Loosely based on the breakdown of her own marriage, it traces the story of Rachel, a cookbook writer who, amid the turmoil of her disintegrating private life, finds emotional salvation in food. On a trip to New York, after she discovers her husband's philandering, she still sees rays of sunshine through her sadness.

"I look out the window and I see the lights and the skyline and the people on the street rushing around looking for action, love, and the world's greatest chocolate chip cookie, and my heart does a little dance."

CHOCOLATE FOR DINNER

"For me, *mole* is very sensual," says Mexican chef and culinary icon Martha Ortiz. "It's so deep and so spicy. The ingredients come from the Old and New Worlds and they are perfect lovers." I am in the kitchen of Ortiz's award-winning restaurant, Dulce Patria, in Mexico City, high on the aroma of spices and chillies. She is teaching me how to make her beloved *mole negro* — a dark version of the famous Mexican sauce, thickened and enriched with chocolate.

For Ortiz, *mole* is hugely symbolic, a celebration of Mexico's rich and vibrant history. Said to be invented by nuns in the city of Puebla in the sixteenth century, one theory states the sister superior wanted to honour a visiting archbishop by blending the ingredients of the New World with the Old, and in the process invented *mole*. Ortiz, who has written several books on regional Mexican cookery, has her own ideas. "My version is that the nuns were so young, their libido had to go somewhere, so it went into the *mole*. The sauce is an ecstasy."

Whether inspired by sexual urges or the desire to impress an archbishop, *mole* is so important at the Mexican table that some people still make it from scratch for festivals and weddings; sometimes, they even bring out the *metate* and grind the ingredients by hand. For everyday cooking, however, ready-made *mole* paste sold at food markets is very good quality and perfectly acceptable. After all, the list of ingredients in *mole* is alarmingly long, at least to a non-Mexican eye.

I have asked Ortiz to show me a simplified version of her *mole negro*, one that I could reproduce in this book for home cooks to replicate. But as I cast my eye over her recipe, which she translated into English for me, I'm worried. Even in its modified form, it still contains dozens of ingredients, including three types of Mexican chocolate, four kinds of chillies (including essential black *chilhuacle* I have never seen outside Mexico) and culinary specialities, such as roasted avocado leaves and charred pepper leaf. What's more, the painstaking method requires countless hours of stirring and simmering.

Later, Ortiz and I share some of the *mole* at a quiet table in her restaurant, and it is indescribably delicious. Although it contains dozens of ingredients, they have been used with such a knowing and delicate hand they don't compete with each other for attention but work together in harmony. I could never do Ortiz's recipe justice by modifying it further for a UK or US kitchen. So, here is my own simple take on *mole*, inspired by the wonderful Chef Martha Ortiz, stirred through slow-cooked pulled pork.

SERVES 8–12

2 whole ancho chillies
2 whole guajillo chillies
2 tsp cumin seeds
2 tsp fennel seeds
2kg/4½lb boneless pork shoulder,
   cut into fist-sized chunks, about
   8cm/3¼in
2 Tbsp flaked sea salt
4 Tbsp pork fat, lard or dripping
   (olive oil is fine), plus extra if needed
2 large white onions, chopped
6 garlic cloves, finely chopped
2 tsp hot chilli powder
1½ Tbsp dried oregano
2 medium ripe tomatoes, chopped

1 Tbsp chipotle chilli flakes or 1 chipotle
   chilli in adobo sauce
2 litres/68fl oz diluted beef stock
6 bay leaves
1 Tbsp red wine vinegar
30g/1oz dark chocolate (100% cocoa
   solids or as high a percentage as you
   can find), grated
salt and freshly ground black pepper
   (optional)

TO SERVE (OPTIONAL)
guacamole
rice or soft bread rolls
chopped tomato salsa
pickled vegetables

Preheat the oven to 170°C/340°F/Gas mark 3.

Cut the whole chillies in half with scissors, discard the stalks and white veins,
and collect the seeds. In a dry frying pan, fry the seeds until dark brown, almost
burnt, then transfer to a spice or coffee grinder or small food processor. Set the
whole chillies aside.

Add the cumin and fennel seeds to the frying pan and fry until toasted and fragrant.
Add to the chilli seeds in the spice grinder and blitz to a powder. Set aside.

Add the reserved whole chillies to the frying pan and fry until the skin is blistered,
turning them over frequently. Transfer to a heatproof bowl, cover with boiling
water (at least 200ml/6¾fl oz) and set aside for 20 minutes.

Meanwhile, pat the pork pieces dry and rub with the salt. Melt the fat in a large
heavy casserole [Dutch oven] over a medium-high heat and fry the pork until
golden brown all over. You will have to do this in batches, so transfer to a bowl
as you go and add more fat if the pan becomes dry. Set the meat aside.

Add the onions to the pan, along with 1 tablespoon more of the fat if needed, then
reduce the heat to low and fry gently until very soft, about 15 minutes. Add the
garlic and cook for a few minutes more.

Add the reserved ground spices and chilli seeds to the onions, along with the chilli powder, oregano and tomatoes. Cook, stirring, over a medium heat for a few minutes until everything is amalgamated and the tomatoes have cooked down a little.

Drain the soaked chillies through a sieve [strainer], reserving the soaking liquid. Transfer to a food processor along with the chipotle chilli flakes (or chilli plus 1 tablespoon of the adobo sauce, if using) and 200ml/6¾fl oz of the chillies soaking liquid and blitz to a smooth paste. Add this to the onions and fry gently for 5 minutes.

Transfer the onion mixture to a large baking tray that has sides 7cm/2¾in deep, add the meat and enough of the stock to almost cover—you want about 1cm/⅜in to poke above the liquid. Tuck in the bay leaves so they are submerged. Set the tray on the hob and bring to the boil, skimming off any scum or fat. Cover tightly with foil and transfer to the oven. Cook for 2½–3 hours until the meat is very soft and can be pulled apart with forks. The top of the meat will have a dark crust and the liquid should be bubbling and a little reduced.

Scoop the meat out of the sauce onto a large serving plate and shred with 2 forks, adding a little of the sauce from the baking tray to moisten. Set the baking tray on the hob [stove] over a medium heat, or pour the sauce into a pan and simmer until reduced and thickened to your liking. Add the vinegar and grated chocolate and simmer for a few more minutes. Taste and add more vinegar, chocolate or salt and pepper.

Pour some of the sauce over the pork and take to the table. Serve the remaining sauce in a jug on the side for guests to help themselves, along with guacamole, rice or soft bread rolls, chopped tomato salsa and pickled vegetables.

POT-ROAST PHEASANT WITH WINE AND SHERRY REDUCTION

Rich game birds demand a deeply flavourful sauce—and this intense reduction is it. Don't use a beef stock cube instead of consommé, as it will be too salty when you reduce it down.

SERVES 2

1 pheasant
1 Tbsp unsalted butter
splash of olive oil
1 red onion, cut into thick rings
1 small carrot, roughly chopped
1 small celery stick, roughly chopped
2 garlic cloves, peeled and crushed
  with the side of a knife
250ml/8½fl oz red wine
250ml/8½fl oz water
2 streaky [lean] bacon rashers [slices],
  unsmoked
sea salt flakes and freshly ground
  black pepper

FOR THE SAUCE

250ml/8½fl oz beef consommé (from
  a can is fine, low salt if possible)
2 Tbsp Pedro Ximénez sherry
1 strip of orange zest
2 juniper berries, crushed
10g/⅓oz dark chocolate (70% cocoa
  solids), chopped
1 Tbsp cold unsalted butter, cubed

TO SERVE

creamy mashed potato
cavolo nero

Preheat the oven to 160°C/325°F/Gas mark 3.

Pat the pheasant dry with paper towels and lightly season inside and out with salt and pepper. Melt the butter and oil in a heavy, lidded casserole [Dutch oven] over a medium heat and brown the pheasant all over. Remove from the pan and set aside.

Pour out and reserve all but 2 Tbsp fat from the pan. Add the onion, carrot, celery and garlic and stir to coat. Cook until softened a little, about 5 minutes, adding some of the reserved fat back in if needed. Place the pheasant on top of the vegetables. Pour the wine and water down the sides of the pan—don't pour it over the top of the bird. Place a bacon rasher on each pheasant breast. Cover the pot and roast until the meat reads 63°C/145°F on a digital probe thermometer stuck into the thickest part of the breast or when the leg meat comes easily away from the bone, around 40 minutes, but the exact time will depend on the bird.

Meanwhile, for the sauce, pour the consommé into a small pan and simmer until it is reduced to 125ml/4¼fl oz. Set aside.

When the pheasant has cooked, remove from the pan and set aside on a plate to rest, loosely covered with foil.

Pour the pan juices through a colander into a jug to separate out the vegetables. Pour 180ml/6fl oz of the strained juices into the pan with the reduced consommé. Add the sherry, orange zest strip, juniper berries and any juices released from the bird, and simmer until reduced to 80–100ml/2¾–3½fl oz. It should be slightly syrupy but don't reduce it too far, or it will be too salty, so keep tasting. With the pan over a low heat, stir in the chocolate and then whisk in the butter to make a rich and glossy sauce.

Serve the pheasant with some of the sauce spooned over and the rest on the side. It's magnificent served with creamy mashed potato and cavolo nero.

RICH AND SPICY TOMATO SOUP

Oven-blasted tomatoes and dark chocolate are very happy companions: they both carry green and roasted aromas and therefore bring out the best in each other. The chocolate smooths out the acidity of the tomatoes, and adds depth and richness to their umami. If you make this soup quite thick you can eat it as a pasta sauce—just stir through spaghetti, linguine or tagliatelle.

SERVES 4

1kg/2¼lb ripe tomatoes
3 Tbsp olive oil
1 Tbsp dried oregano
1 red onion, finely chopped
1 medium carrot, finely chopped
1 celery stick, finely chopped
1 fat garlic clove, finely chopped

2 Tbsp rose harissa paste
600ml/21fl oz chicken or vegetable stock
30g/1oz dark chocolate (70% cocoa
  solids), chopped
1 tsp balsamic vinegar
sea salt flakes and freshly ground
  black pepper

Preheat the oven to 190°C/375°F/Gas mark 5.

Cut the tomatoes in half horizontally and place cut-side up in a roasting tray. Drizzle with 1 tablespoon of the oil and sprinkle with the oregano and ½ teaspoon salt and some black pepper. Roast for 1 hour–1 hour 15 minutes until tender and slightly charred at the edges.

Meanwhile, heat the remaining oil in a pan over a medium-low heat, add the onion, carrot, celery and a pinch of salt and gently fry for 15 minutes, or until very soft and tender. Stir the garlic into the vegetables, along with the harissa paste, and fry for a further 2 minutes, stirring everything well. Remove the pan from the heat and set aside until the tomatoes have finished roasting.

Transfer the tomatoes and tray juices to the pan with the vegetables. There will be lots of caramelized bits in the bottom of the tray—this is flavour!—so deglaze it. To do this, set the tray over a medium-high heat, add half the stock, and scrape off the caramelized bits as it bubbles away. Pour the contents of the tray and the rest of the stock into the pan with the tomatoes. Simmer gently for 25 minutes, or until the liquid has reduced slightly and the tomatoes are falling apart.

Blitz the tomato mixture in a blender or use a stick blender until smooth and then return to the pan. If the soup is too thick, add a little water, then add the chocolate and stir until melted. Add half the balsamic vinegar and have a taste: the soup should have a little bit of acidity, bitterness and sweetness, so gradually add more vinegar until it tastes good to you. Serve hot.

PASTA WITH GORGONZOLA, WALNUTS, ROSEMARY AND CHOCOLATE

Many people forget that it is only the addition of sugar that makes chocolate sweet — imaginative cooks, especially in Italy, have been using it as a spice for centuries, including in pasta. The chocolate imparts a delicate bitterness that works beautifully with Gorgonzola, or with a sage, butter and Parmesan sauce, or even with chopped and fried bacon or porcini.

SERVES 2

30g/1oz walnuts
220g/7¾oz dried tagliatelle
1 Tbsp unsalted butter
2 fat garlic cloves, finely chopped
1 Tbsp rosemary leaves, finely chopped
80ml/2¾fl oz double [heavy] cream
3 Tbsp dry white wine
100g/3½oz Gorgonzola, chopped,
  plus extra (chopped) to serve

40g/1½oz Parmesan cheese, grated
finely grated zest of ½ lemon
salt and freshly ground black pepper
dark chocolate (100% cocoa solids),
  for grating, or about ½ tsp cacao nibs,
  finely blitzed in a spice grinder, to serve

Preheat the oven to 180°C/350°F/Gas mark 4. Spread the walnuts out on a baking sheet and roast for 10 minutes, shaking the sheet halfway through, until lightly toasted. When cool enough to handle, roughly chop.

While the nuts are roasting, prepare the pasta and sauce. Cook the tagliatelle in a large pan of boiling salted water for 1 minute less than the packet instructions.

Meanwhile, place the butter, garlic and rosemary in a small frying pan and cook over a medium-low heat until everything is gently sizzling and smelling delicious. Be careful not to burn the garlic.

Add the cream, wine and 60ml/2fl oz of the pasta cooking water and gently bubble away for a minute or so. Add the Gorgonzola and Parmesan and cook gently, stirring, until the cheese has melted. Add more pasta water if needed to make a loose but creamy sauce. Add the lemon zest and a good grinding of black pepper. Taste and add more salt or pepper if you like.

When the pasta is cooked, lightly drain, reserving a good splosh of the cooking water, and return the pasta to the pan. Add the sauce and quickly toss together, then fold in most of the roasted nuts, adding a little of the reserved pasta water if necessary to loosen.

Serve topped with more Gorgonzola, the remaining walnuts and a generous grating of chocolate or finely blitzed cacao nibs.

COPPA WITH BITTER LEAVES, FIGS AND NIB VINAIGRETTE

This makes a very pretty, flavourful starter—the chocolate notes are very gentle because it's being used as a spice. Opt for cacao nibs in the dressing instead of the 100% dark chocolate if you prefer. I love the tiny nuggets of flavour and texture, but some people aren't so sure. It's easy to buy 100% dark chocolate these days, but if you can't, just use the highest cocoa content chocolate you can find. Avoid cocoa powder, as it's too harsh and bitter.

SERVES 2 AS A STARTER [APPETIZER]
15g/½oz skinless hazelnuts
4–6 purple endive leaves or pink
  (castelfranco) radicchio
4–6 slices coppa (about 40g/1½oz)
  or prosciutto
2 large ripe figs, quartered

FOR THE DRESSING
2½ tsp grated dark chocolate (100%
  cocoa solids) or crushed cacao nibs
3 Tbsp extra virgin olive oil
1 Tbsp hazelnut oil (extra virgin olive
  oil is fine)
2 Tbsp good-quality balsamic vinegar
½ tsp finely grated orange zest, or more
  to taste
sea salt flakes and freshly ground
  black pepper

Preheat the oven to 180°C/350°F/Gas mark 4.

Place all the dressing ingredients in a screw-top jar, close and shake well. Set aside for the flavours to get to know each other and then taste, adding a little more orange zest or salt and pepper if needed.

Spread the hazelnuts out on a rimmed baking sheet and roast for about 12 minutes, or until pale gold. Be careful not to let them go too dark, or the salad will taste bitter. When cool enough to handle, roughly chop.

Arrange the endive or radicchio in the centre of 2 plates and top with the coppa slices and fig quarters. Drizzle over the dressing—you'll want to use all of it— and scatter with the hazelnuts. Serve immediately.

CAPONATA

Caponata is the embodiment of Sicily, a celebration of sun-ripened vegetables made truly splendid (in the Baroque style of its dazzling cities) with bold sweet and sour *agrodolce* flavours. Chocolate is not always added to caponata, but often is. It's a good example of Spain—which 'discovered' chocolate in the New World—leaving its fingerprints on the cuisine of the island it controlled for centuries. Serve with grilled prawns, or juicy lamb steaks marinated in olive oil, garlic and lemon zest and cooked on a barbecue. It's equally delicious served on good toasted bread, and/or with a creamy orb of burrata on top.

SERVES 6

2 medium aubergines [eggplants], about 700g/1lb 9oz in total
1 tsp fine sea salt
olive oil or vegetable oil, for frying
120ml/4fl oz extra virgin olive oil
1 red onion, chopped
2 celery sticks, chopped small
2 ripe tomatoes, chopped
200ml/6¾fl oz passata [strained tomatoes]

60ml/2fl oz red wine vinegar
4 Tbsp capers, rinsed and drained if salted
40g/1½oz sultanas [golden raisins]
15g/½oz dark chocolate (between 70–80% cocoa solids), chopped
1 tsp caster [superfine] sugar
sea salt flakes and freshly ground black pepper
1 small handful each of basil and mint leaves

Cut the aubergines into 1-cm/⅜-in cubes. Transfer to a colander, toss with the fine sea salt and set over a sink or bowl to drain for about 20 minutes. Squeeze out any excess liquid and pat dry with paper towels.

Fill a deep pan around 2cm/¾in up the sides with the frying oil and, when hot (a cube of aubergine should sizzle and dance), fry the aubergines in batches until golden all over. You will need to keep adjusting the heat, so the cubes are golden and cooked through. Transfer to a plate lined with paper towels as you go.

Heat the extra virgin olive oil in a large frying pan over a low heat, add the onion, celery and a good pinch of salt and cook gently for 10 minutes until very soft but not coloured. Add the tomatoes and passata and cook for a further 5–10 minutes until the tomatoes have cooked down into a thick tomato sauce. Taste, and add salt and pepper until the flavours are nicely balanced. Remove the pan from the heat and stir in the vinegar, capers, sultanas, chocolate and sugar. Return to a low heat, cover and cook for 10–15 minutes until you have a thick stew. Taste and add more salt, pepper, sugar or vinegar. You should have a punchy stew with a balance of sweet, sour and savoury. Set aside for at least a few hours to let all the flavours develop and mellow. Sprinkle the basil and mint over the top just before serving.

Dolceforte, literally meaning 'sweet and strong' in Italian, has been a popular style of sauce for meat since the sixteenth century, when chefs in Florence began experimenting with cacao in cooking. Comprising raisins, pine nuts, dark chocolate, candied fruit and vinegar, it makes a complex sauce that works especially well with game. Different variations can be found in Tuscany, as well as in Spain. I've used rabbit here, but the sauce also works well with venison, wild boar and all kinds of game birds; it's even served with tongue and dried salt cod. The sweetness of the fruit and chocolate and the bitterness of the vinegar is a fantastic foil to the richness of the meat.

SERVES 2 GENEROUSLY

1 wild rabbit, jointed
olive oil, for frying
75g/2¾oz pancetta, cubed
1 medium carrot, finely chopped
1 celery stick, finely chopped
½ white onion, finely chopped
1 Tbsp plain [all-purpose] flour
200ml/6¾fl oz red wine
400ml/13½fl oz dilute chicken stock
1 bay leaf
1 rosemary sprig

25g/1oz sultanas [golden raisins]
25g/1oz dried cherries
25g/1oz pine nuts
25g/1oz dark chocolate (70% cocoa
  solids), chopped
1 Tbsp white wine vinegar, plus more
  to taste
salt and freshly ground black pepper

TO SERVE

good-quality bread
green salad or cooked greens

Pat the rabbit dry with paper towels and season generously with salt and pepper. Set aside.

Heat a splash of olive oil in a frying pan large enough to accommodate the rabbit snugly in a single layer. Add the pancetta and gently fry until golden and the fat has rendered. Remove from the pan with a slotted spoon and set aside.

Lightly brown the rabbit pieces all over in the same pan. Work in batches if necessary so you don't overcrowd the pan: you want the pieces to sear, not steam. When browned, transfer to a plate.

Pour a splash more oil into the pan (if there isn't enough fat left), add the carrot, celery and onion, and season generously with salt and pepper. Gently fry over a medium-low heat until the vegetables are very soft, about 15–20 minutes.

Sprinkle over the flour and stir for a minute or so. Return the pancetta to the pan and pour in the wine, scraping the bottom of the pan to loosen any caramelized bits. Add the rabbit pieces in a single layer and then enough stock to just cover (top up with water if necessary). Tuck in the bay leaf and rosemary sprig. Bring to a gentle simmer, then reduce the heat to low and cover, leaving the lid slightly ajar if it doesn't have a steam hole. Cook very gently for 1 hour 45 minutes, or until tender (it might take longer than this depending on the rabbit), turning over now and then.

Meanwhile, place the sultanas and cherries in a small bowl and just cover with boiling water. Set aside until the rabbit has cooked.

Drain the dried fruit and add to the pan with the pine nuts, chocolate and vinegar. Stir well so everything is combined, then gently simmer, uncovered, for 15 minutes, spooning the sauce over the rabbit frequently, until thickened. Taste and add more salt, pepper or vinegar if you wish: there should be a pleasing balance of sweet and bitter. Serve hot with good bread and a green salad or cooked greens.

BEEF CHEEK AND BONE MARROW POT PIE

Bone marrow is wonderfully rich and delicious and adds extra decadence to a meaty pie enriched with chocolate. Marrow bones are widely available online and from good butchers.

Serve this pie with a crisp green salad daubed with a sharp dressing—and a jar of pickles on the side.

SERVES 6

about 1kg/2¼lb beef or ox cheeks, approximately 2 cheeks, cut into 2-cm/¾-in chunks

250ml/8½fl oz red wine

4 fat garlic cloves, peeled and crushed with the side of a knife

3 thyme sprigs

4 bay leaves

1 × 10-cm/4-in marrowbone, cut in half horizontally (ask your butcher to do this)

2 Tbsp olive oil, or more if needed

sea salt flakes and freshly ground black pepper

3 Tbsp lard, plus extra if needed

1 celery stick, finely sliced

2 carrots, finely chopped

1 onion, finely chopped

300g/10½oz ripe tomatoes, finely chopped

about 500ml/17fl oz hot beef stock, plus more if needed

40g/1½oz dark chocolate (70% cocoa solids), finely chopped

½ tsp ground white pepper

1 Tbsp red wine vinegar, plus extra to taste

1 sheet ready-rolled puff pastry or 320g/11¼oz block

plain [all-purpose] flour, for dusting (optional)

1 egg, lightly beaten with a splash of milk, for egg wash

Place the meat in a large non-reactive bowl (glass or plastic but not metal) and add the red wine, garlic, thyme and bay leaves. Make sure the meat is immersed as far as possible, and the herbs and garlic are tucked underneath. Cover with plastic wrap and marinate in the fridge for at least 1 hour, or overnight if possible.

When you're ready to cook the pie, preheat the oven to 220°C/425°F/Gas mark 7.

Place the marrowbone halves in a roasting tray, cut-side up, drizzle with 1 tablespoon of the olive oil and roast for about 30 minutes, or until golden. Set aside and reduce the oven temperature to 160°C/325°F/Gas mark 3.

Drain the meat and reserve the marinade, garlic and herbs. Pat the meat dry with paper towels and season generously with salt and pepper.

Heat half the lard in a heavy, lidded casserole (a Dutch oven is perfect) over a medium-high heat and brown the meat in batches, adding more lard as needed. Don't crowd the pan or the meat will steam. Transfer to a bowl with a slotted spoon as you go.

Reduce the heat to medium-low and add the remaining olive oil (omit this if there's enough fat left in the pan). Add the celery, carrots and onion, season well with salt and pepper and cook gently, stirring now and then, until very soft, about 10 minutes.

Return the meat to the pan along with the reserved marinade, garlic and herbs, and the tomatoes. Stir well, so everything is combined, scraping up any bits stuck to the bottom of the pan. Pour in enough of the stock to just cover the meat, and simmer for a minute or so. Remove the pan from the heat, place the marrowbone halves on top, cut-side down, and cover. Transfer to the oven and cook for 2 hours, stirring halfway through, until the meat is very tender.

When cooked, remove the pan from the oven and increase the temperature to 220°C/425°F/Gas mark 7. Remove the marrowbones and set aside. Pour the meat, vegetables and juices through a large sieve [strainer] or colander, catching the juices in a large jug or bowl. Return the meat and vegetables to the casserole. Pour the juices into a medium pan. Scoop the marrow out of the bones with a spoon, finely chop and add to the pan with the juices, along with the chocolate, white pepper and vinegar. Gently simmer until thickened and reduced by about one-third. Taste and add more salt, pepper or vinegar, if you like. Pour over the meat, stir and set aside to cool for 10 minutes.

Using a slotted spoon, scoop the meat into a 20-cm/8-in pie dish. Don't add any more juice than that clinging to the meat and vegetables, or there will be too much liquid in the pie.

If using a block of pastry, roll it out on a lightly floured work surface to 3mm/⅛in thick. Cut a disc of pastry 23cm/9in in diameter and a strip/strips of pastry 3cm wide and long enough to cover the rim of your pie dish.

Brush the rim of the pie dish with egg wash and place the strip/s of pastry on top, gently pressing it down so it sticks. Place the disc of pastry on top, gently pressing it onto the strip. Fold any pastry overhang over to make a double layer of crust around the edge, and neatly crimp.

Make 3 small slits in the centre of the pastry or use a pie funnel to let the steam out and brush with egg wash. Bake for 20–25 minutes until puffed and golden.

STICKY SLOW-ROASTED BEEF SHORT RIBS WITH COCOA AND MAPLE

Give me succulent slow-cooked short ribs slicked with sauce over standard roast meat any day: the flavour is unbeatable, especially served with this chocolate-laced sauce, as the cocoa augments the roasted notes of the meat.

SERVES 4

1.2kg/2½lb beef short ribs on the bone

2 Tbsp lard or olive oil

4 Tbsp maple syrup, or to taste
  (use mild honey at a pinch)

10g/⅓oz dark chocolate (70% cocoa
  solids), chopped

sea salt flakes and freshly ground
  black pepper

soft polenta or creamy mashed potato,
  to serve

FOR THE MARINADE

500ml/17fl oz German-style wheat beer,
  ideally Dunkelweizen

2 rosemary sprigs

3 garlic cloves, peeled and bruised
  with the side of a knife

3 bay leaves

1 Tbsp cocoa powder

1 Tbsp smoked paprika

sea salt flakes and freshly ground
  black pepper

Place all the marinade ingredients in a plastic lidded container that will hold the ribs snugly and stir to combine. Add the ribs, turning to coat in the marinade, cover, then chill overnight, turning the ribs over halfway through.

To cook the ribs, preheat the oven to 160°C/325°F/Gas mark 3. Remove the ribs from the marinade and pat dry with paper towels. Pour the marinade, herbs and garlic into a roasting tray that fit the ribs snugly. (If you use a roasting tray that's too large, the marinade will spread too thinly and evaporate.)

Heat the lard or oil in a frying pan over a medium-high heat and brown the ribs well on all sides. Transfer to the marinade in the roasting tray, then cover tightly with a double layer of foil. Roast for 1 hour 30 minutes–2 hours until the meat is very tender and falling off the bone. Remove from the oven and leave the oven on.

Remove the ribs from the marinade and set aside. Pour the marinade into a pan and simmer until reduced to 150ml/5fl oz. Stir in the maple syrup and chocolate until melted. Taste and season with salt and pepper, adding more maple syrup, if necessary (some wheat beers are more bitter than others).

Place the ribs on a rack set over a rimmed baking sheet and brush all over with the marinade. Return to the oven and cook for a further 20 minutes or so, frequently basting the ribs with more of the marinade during cooking, until sticky.

Serve with the rest of the marinade, on soft polenta or creamy mashed potatoes, with some mouth-puckering gherkins if you like.

SOFT CHEESE SALAD WITH BLACKBERRIES, MINT AND NIBS

This is a fresh and bright salad, positively thrumming with flavour due in part to the cocoa notes and crunch of the nibs. It's also hearty, too, thanks to the cheese. With some good bread on the side this could just as easily be served as an excellent light lunch as a starter [appetizer], and very pretty it is too. Use a good mix of baby leaves and soft herbs that provide a range of bitter and sweet flavours—it will make all the difference.

SERVES 2
50g/1¾oz mixed baby salad leaves
15 large mint leaves, finely sliced
60g/2¼oz ripe blackberries, large
  ones halved
50g/1¾oz mild soft goat's cheese
  or Brillat-Savarin
1 Tbsp cacao nibs, lightly crushed
  with a rolling pin

FOR THE DRESSING
4 Tbsp extra virgin olive oil
1 Tbsp blackberry vinegar or similar
  berry vinegar
pinch of mustard powder
sea salt flakes and freshly ground
  black pepper

Start by making the salad dressing. Simply place all the ingredients in a screw-top jar, close and shake well.

Combine the salad leaves, half the mint, and the blackberries in a bowl and toss gently with enough of the dressing to lightly coat, but not drown the leaves.

Divide the salad between serving plates, then dot with the cheese. Drizzle over more of the dressing and scatter with the cacao nibs and remaining mint. Serve immediately.

"It may need an act of faith to include the chocolate, but please don't leave it out." —Jane Grigson, *Good Things* (1971)

In the early 2000s, when the food world was developing a fetish for alarming flavour combinations, I watched a short film in a series by the Royal Society of Chemistry called *Kitchen Chemistry*, presented by a wide-eyed, going-places chef by the name of Heston Blumenthal. In the film, Heston explained how to make a French dessert called *chocolat coulant*—a pudding with an oozing centre made from chocolate and—sound the clarions!—blue cheese. Curious about what kind of sorcery this was, I made it, and to my surprise it was delicious.

Food scientists and molecular gastronomists can explain why this oddball pairing (at least it was considered such back then) works so well. Blue cheese and chocolate have more than 60 aroma molecules in common; like good marriages, the two bring out the best in each other in surprisingly lovely ways. And because chocolate boasts one of the most complex flavour profiles of any food, with more than 600 known aroma molecules, it pairs well with a panoply of ingredients, many more than most home cooks and chefs consider.

Moreover, chocolate is only sweet because of the addition of sugar. In its natural form, cacao tastes bitter and also boasts a rainbow of subtle flavours that work beautifully in savoury as well as sweet dishes. Just like other seeds commonly used in cooking, such as black pepper, fennel, cardamom and caraway, cacao can bring welcome bright notes, contrast and complexity to all sorts of non-sweet dishes, especially rich ones. Just a square or two of dark chocolate can add an indefinable richness as well as deliciousness —without any overbearing sweetness—to sauces and stews, like an unseen hand working culinary magic in the pan.

Chocolate scholars disagree about when cacao first made its way on to dining tables, as distinct from into drinks. Sophie and

Michael Coe, authors of *The True History of Chocolate*, argue there is no evidence the Aztecs ever used chocolate in food, and that the very idea would have horrified them. The Aztecs regarded cacao as a sacred ingredient bestowed on them by the gods, and as such it commanded a special place in ceremonies and rituals associated with birth, coming of age, marriage and death. For the Aztecs to have cooked with cacao, the Coes argue, would be like preparing coq au vin with communion wine today.

Other experts disagree. Archaeologists have found traces of cacao alongside turkey and fish remains in ceramic vessels and on fragments unearthed in ancient royal tombs in Honduras. A platter typically used to serve *tamales,* a savoury dish cooked in corn husks, also carried traces of cacao residue. In the Yucatan peninsula in Mexico, traces of 2,500-year-old cacao have been found on a plate, suggesting the precious ingredient might have been used as a condiment or sauce for food. Perhaps these cacao-spiked meals were revered as divine nourishment, just as chocolate drinks were considered sacred?

One of the most famous of all savoury dishes containing chocolate is *mole poblano*, a version of the classic Mexican sauce traditionally served with turkey. One legend holds that the dish dates back to the sixteenth century, when nuns of the Santa Rosa convent in the Mexican city Puebla were preparing a dish for a visiting bishop and added chocolate by accident. Another tale states that nuns deliberately concocted the sauce for a visiting Spanish dignitary; to celebrate the coming together of Old and New Worlds, they united European and indigenous ingredients in the same pot. Again, no evidence exists to support the stories, but there might be some truth to them. The name *mole* derives from the Aztec word for sauce, *molli*. Perhaps the nuns added New World spices like cinnamon and cloves to an Old World sauce that on occasion included cacao, in order to create something new and special in honour of their guests.

Whatever *mole poblano*'s origins, soon after its rumoured invention in Mexico, savoury dishes containing chocolate began to appear on the grandest tables in Europe, and in recipe books. Chocolate arrived in Spain in the mid-sixteenth century and quickly became fashionable among the rich and powerful as a drink, and eventually in cooking, notably in the cuisine of Catalonia. Chocolate is still used as a flavour component in a number of Catalan specialities that date back centuries to a time when the region, situated in the heart of the Mediterranean, was rich from trading and its cooking influenced by French and Italian merchants.

Picada, one of the base sauces of Catalan cuisine, is usually made with ground garlic, almonds, fried bread, olive oil and sometimes chocolate. The sauce is often stirred into a dish towards the end of cooking to thicken and round out the flavours, for example in *calamars farcits amb salsa xocolata* (squid with chocolate sauce). Chocolate is also added to *llebre amb xocolata* (hare with almonds and chocolate), one of the most famous dishes of the Catalan kitchen, according to food writer Elisabeth Luard. In her book *The Food of Spain and Portugal*, she explains this rich dark stew is thickened 'in the Italian manner' with dark chocolate.

Seventeenth-century Italian chefs working in the grandest houses and palaces were eager to demonstrate their culinary showmanship with chocolate, an ingredient only the very wealthy could afford. Italian food expert and historian Francine Segan says savoury dishes containing chocolate were first published as far back as 1680. By 1736 chocolate was popping up in so many weird and wonderful guises that poet Francesco Arisi was moved to pen *Il Cioccolato*, in which he mocks the many crimes against chocolate, including cooks who 'imprison' it in pastilles and meat pastries.

Chocolate certainly inspired Italian chefs to give full throttle to their imaginations, and Sophie and Michael Coe cite several intriguing examples from the eighteenth century. A 1786 manuscript from Macerata, in the Marche region, mentions lasagne made with a sauce of almonds, anchovies, walnuts and cocoa. A list of meals served to magistrates in the Tuscan city of Lucca includes *pappardelle di cioccolato,* pasta ribbons made with cocoa. And from Trento, in the foothills of the Alps, priest Don Felici Libera proposed delights such as pan-fried chocolate-coated liver, polenta cooked with chocolate breadcrumbs and chocolate pudding with veal marrow.

One of Italy's most famous chocolate-scented savoury dishes is *cinghiale dolceforte* (wild boar cooked in a 'sweet and strong' sauce) from Tuscany, which appears in Pellegrino Artusi's 1891 cookbook *Science in the Kitchen and the Art of Eating Well*. The recipe instructs that meat and vegetables should be simmered in water, and then a divinely rich sauce made from raisins, pine nuts, candied fruit, sugar and chocolate stirred in at the end, just like a Catalan *picada*. Beef, hare and tongue are still prepared this way in Tuscany, often with vinegar and wine added. Grigson's recipe for sweet-sour rabbit Italian-style, with chocolate, in which she implores English readers not to leave the chocolate out, is a variation on the theme.

Sicily's long connection with chocolate has also produced some tantalizing cocoa-imbued savoury dishes. In some parts of the island, chocolate is added as a flourish to the vegetable stew, *caponata* (page 212), as well as to pork ragout, a speciality of Enna, which is served during the Christmas holidays. A very old dish, *teste di Turco* (Turkish heads), comprises pork and ricotta pies topped with swirls of cocoa meringue, designed to look like turbans, perhaps a nod to the island's Arab heritage.

Some Italian desserts made with chocolate have a savoury element. In Campania, *melanzane al cioccolato* (aubergine with chocolate), thought to originate in the region's monasteries, is often prepared for the holy day of Ferragosto, or Assumption Day, when Catholics believe the Virgin Mary was taken into heaven. Chocolate also has a connection with blood in Italy, perhaps mirroring the significance of chocolate drinks as a symbol of human blood in Aztec civilization. At one time in Italy, pig's blood was considered sacred, as well as highly nutritious, and was combined with chocolate to make blood sausages (*sanguinaccio*) after the ritual slaughter of the animals. In communities where pigs are still reared and slaughtered, these sausages continue to be made, and also *sanguinaccio dolce*, a creamy custard-style pudding made with pig's blood, chocolate, candied fruit and spices.

But despite its fashionability for a time, chocolate never really caught on in savoury cooking. This is probably due to the fact chocolate was astronomically expensive in the seventeenth and eighteenth centuries, and hard to come by during the Napoleonic wars, when cocoa imports to Europe were blocked. Meals garlanded with chocolate were simply out of reach for anyone except the extremely wealthy, or reserved for special occasions. Interestingly, savoury dishes perfumed with chocolate have started reappearing on restaurant menus over recent decades, prepared by chefs who probably believe they are bringing something innovative to the table. I wonder how many realize that the combination is, in fact, as old as chocolate itself?

RECIPE

One of the oldest recorded recipes for a savoury dish containing chocolate dates to 1691, when chef to the French royal family and aristocracy, François Massialot, published *Le cuisinier roïal et bourgeois,* a guide to preparing meals for the upper classes. In it he offered a recipe for *Macreuse en ragoût au chocolat:* sea duck poached in a chocolate broth, served with a rich mushroom, truffle and chestnut stew.

MACREUSE EN RAGOÛT AU CHOCOLAT (SEA DUCK WITH CHOCOLATE STEW)

Having plucked and cleaned your Sea Duck, gut it and wash it, precook it over embers and then poach it in broth and season it with salt, pepper, and a bouquet [of fines herbs]. Make a little chocolate and throw it in. At the same time, make a stew with liver, white mushrooms, morels, Fairy Rings [a wild forest mushroom], truffles, [and] a handful of chestnuts; and, your Macreuse cooked and dressed in a plate, pour the stew on it and serve with whatever accompaniment you like. Recipe by François Massialot, published in *Le cuisinier roïal et bourgeois*, 1691

SALT AND CHOCOLATE

Salt heightens the flavour of most foods, but works particular magic with chocolate. If you use it regularly in chocolate dishes, you really notice its absence if you leave it out. This is because salt is the one basic taste missing from unflavoured sweetened chocolate; adding some emphasizes the cocoa notes and gives them clarity. It's a good rule of thumb to have the salt pot nearby whenever you are cooking with chocolate.

Chocolate really does seem to pair with just about anything, so
I talked to chefs, scoured cookbooks, reference books and flavour
wheels, and drew on my own cooking experience, to identify some
delicious chocolate partnerships.

FRUIT

Apricots, bananas, cherries, coconut, figs, lemon, lime, bergamot, orange
(sweet and bitter), pears, apples, strawberry, pineapple, berries, rhubarb,
mango, tomato, cranberry, passionfruit, plums, dried fruit (prunes, dates,
figs, raisins)

VEGETABLES

Aubergine, avocado, beetroot, black truffle, olives, mushrooms, cauliflower

NUTS AND SEEDS

Almonds, cashews, hazelnuts, macadamias, peanuts (and peanut butter),
walnuts, pecans, pistachios, chestnuts, sesame seeds (white and black)

FLOWERS AND HERBS

Mint, rosemary, thyme, basil, bay leaf, sage, rose, orange blossom, lavender

SPICES

Anise/fennel, cardamom, chilli, cinnamon, ginger, nutmeg, saffron, pink
peppercorns, black peppercorns, Szechuan pepper, sumac, cumin seeds,
coriander seeds

DAIRY

Blue cheese, goat's cheese, Gruyère, Emmental, Parmesan, milk, cream,
butter, yogurt, mascarpone, ricotta

MISCELLANEOUS

Crispy bacon, roast and braised meat (beef, chicken, pork and game),
honey, balsamic vinegar, caramel, toffee, brown sugar, malt, maple
syrup, molasses, prawns, marzipan, coffee, tea (black, Earl Grey,
lapsang souchong)

ALCOHOL

Porter, stout, rum, Pedro Ximénez sherry, marsala, Muscat, rum,
bourbon, red wine, fruit liqueurs, chocolate liqueurs, port, brandy,
Frangelico, Grand Marnier, Mezcal, Cognac

A BOX OF CHOCOLATES

CHOCOLATE AND CHILLI POPCORN

I devoured a whole bowl of these addictive morsels on my own in the bar of Mexican chef Martha Ortiz's London restaurant, Ella Canta. She serves them as a bar snack, and they are wonderful washed down with *aqua fresca*, refreshing non-alcoholic drinks made from blended fruit and water. This is Martha's recipe, which she has kindly shared.

If you are feeding a crowd you might want to make several batches, but this is the amount I like to cook at one time, so as not to burn the popcorn.

SERVES 4 PER BATCH

50g/1¾oz popcorn kernels
2 Tbsp vegetable oil (olive oil is fine)
50g/1¾oz caster [superfine] sugar
2 Tbsp liquid glucose
3 Tbsp cocoa powder

4 Tbsp unsalted butter
¼ tsp vanilla extract
⅛ tsp (generous pinch of) sea salt flakes
⅛ tsp (generous pinch of) hot ancho or other chilli powder

Preheat the oven to 120°C/250°F/Gas mark ½ and line a rimmed baking sheet with baking paper. Set aside.

You can pop the popcorn according to the packet instructions, or your favourite method, but this is the way I do it. Place the corn kernels and oil in a heavy, lidded pan, large enough to accommodate the kernels easily in a single layer. Stir to coat in the oil, set the pan over a medium-high heat and cover. As soon as you hear the kernels start to pop, wearing oven gloves, carefully give the pan a good shake, ideally up and down while holding the lid on. Return the pan to the heat and cook, shaking now and then, until the corn stops popping. Remove the pan from the heat and transfer the popcorn to a heatproof bowl.

Place the sugar, liquid glucose, cocoa and butter in a small pan over a medium-high heat and stir until the butter melts and the sugar dissolves. Simmer very gently for 1 minute: the mixture will thicken slightly, but too much and it will turn to caramel. Remove the pan from the heat and stir in the vanilla. Pour the chocolate over the popcorn, then using a rubber spatula, mix so the popcorn is coated in the chocolate, pressing down gently and scraping the bottom of the bowl as you go. Continue until most of the popcorn is coated.

Spread the popcorn out in a single layer on the prepared baking sheet, pressing down to flatten any clumps. Sprinkle with the salt and chilli powder. Bake for 30 minutes, stirring several times. Remove from the oven, and allow to cool to room temperature. Break into small clumps and store in an airtight container.

Chocolate is a tasty canvas on which to let loose your artistic streak — and to experiment pairing cocoa with interesting flavours and textures. This isn't a recipe per se, rather a guide to making shards of beautifully decorated chocolate.

Before you start, decide what kind of toppings you would like to decorate your bark with, and have them ready, as you need to add them before the melted chocolate sets. I've listed some of my favourites below.

For shiny bark with a perfect finish and snap, melt the chocolate using the hairdryer method on page 43 to keep it in temper. Alternatively, simply melt the chocolate as instructed and store the bark in the fridge.

seeds

salt crystals, crushed peppercorns
    and chilli [red pepper] flakes

freeze-dried fruits and powders,
    especially raspberry, strawberry
    and passionfruit

chopped nuts, including green
    pistachios for vibrant colour

dried edible flowers for texture
    and colour, such as cornflowers,
    rose, calendula

chopped dried fruit, including unusual
    ones such as barberries and dried
    cranberries

chopped stem [preserved] ginger
    and crystallized [candied] fruit

savoury morsels, such as chopped
    pretzels, crackers and potato crisps

chopped sweet cookies and biscuits

toasted sourdough breadcrumbs or
    toasted coconut flakes

chopped sweets [candies] and sprinkles,
    such as liquorice allsorts, Smarties
    and marshmallows

Butter a large rimmed baking sheet or roasting tray and line with baking paper — the butter will help it stay in place. Melt 600g/21oz dark chocolate (no more than 70% cocoa solids) following the tempering instructions on page 43. Alternatively, slowly melt the same quantity of chopped chocolate in a heatproof bowl set over a pan of barely simmering water, making sure the bottom of the bowl doesn't touch the water.

Pour the melted chocolate into the prepared tray, tilting it so it spreads into the corners. While it is still soft, add the toppings of your choice. Leave to set completely before breaking into shards.

CHOCOLATE AND BLACK SALT CARAMELS

If you're into making edible gifts or love caramels, these are a winner. I concede that black lava salt from Hawaii, shiny black mineral-rich flakes made from sea salt and activated charcoal, is not a condiment sitting in everyone's pantry. But the distinctive briny, mineral-flavoured flecks add delicious crunch to everything from eggs to bread, so it's worth seeking them out at health food shops or online. If this isn't possible, just use any other really good plain or smoked sea salt flakes.

MAKES ABOUT 64
150g/5¼oz dark chocolate (between
  50–60% cocoa solids), finely chopped
  or grated
400ml/13½fl oz double [heavy] cream
400g/14oz granulated sugar
230g/8oz golden [corn] syrup
45g/1½oz unsalted butter
60ml/2fl oz water
black lava salt, to taste

Line a 20 × 20-cm/8 × 8-in baking dish or brownie tin with baking paper, making slits in the corners so it fits neatly. Let the paper overhang the sides.

Place the chocolate in a heatproof bowl and have it ready by the hob [stove]. Heat the cream in a pan until almost boiling, then pour it over the chocolate, stirring constantly, until melted and well combined. Set aside.

Place all the remaining ingredients, except the salt, in a deep heavy pan. Mix well so that everything is moistened. Set the pan over a medium-high heat and simmer without stirring, just swirling the pan now and then, until the temperature reaches 125°C/257°F on a sugar thermometer. Remove the pan from the heat and very slowly and carefully pour the chocolate cream into the caramel, stirring all the time—watch out, as it will froth up. Return the pan to the heat and simmer, stirring now and then, until the mixture returns to 125°C/257°F.

Pour the mixture into the prepared baking dish and leave to cool for 10 minutes. Sprinkle the top with salt, then leave to cool and set. This might take a few hours or even overnight.

When set, lift out using the baking paper as handles onto a chopping [cutting] board and cut into small squares or rectangles, then wrap in baking paper. These can be kept for up to 6 months but don't store in the fridge.

Sticky, chewy and subtly chocolaty, these are delicious bites to have in the picnic hamper, or restorative snacks for the backpack on a long walk. Keep them at arm's length if, like me, restraint isn't one of your virtues.

MAKES 36 × 4-CM / 10-IN SQUARES
80g / 2¾oz white sesame seeds
80g / 2¾oz hazelnuts, finely chopped
40g / 1½oz cacao nibs, finely chopped
80g / 2¾oz pitted dates, finely chopped
170g / 6oz caster [superfine] sugar
120g / 4¼oz runny honey
2 pinches of ground cinnamon
2 pinches of ground nutmeg
1 Tbsp water

Have 2 large squares of baking paper ready.

Mix the sesame seeds, hazelnuts, nibs and dates together in a bowl so everything is evenly distributed.

In a heavy pan, mix the sugar, honey, cinnamon, nutmeg and water together. Slowly bring to the boil, shaking the pan now and then but not stirring, and boil for 2 minutes. Pour a few drops into a glass of cold water. If it hardens it's ready, if not, keep cooking, checking every 30 seconds or so.

When ready, remove the pan from the heat and stir in the seeds, nuts, dates and nibs. Working quickly, pour the mixture out onto the sheet of baking paper, place the second sheet on top and use a rolling pin to roll out to 3mm / ⅛in thick. Very carefully peel back the top sheet of paper: the mixture is still sticky.

Leave to cool for 10 minutes, then use a pizza cutter or knife to cut into 4-cm / 10-in squares. Leave to harden and cool completely, about 1 hour.

ROSE PETAL AND CACAO NIB JAM

I urge you to make this jam, not only because it's delicious and pretty as a picture spread on toast or spooned over thick Greek yogurt but because your kitchen will smell ambrosial as you make it. It is a sweet and obviously highly perfumed jam, so the cacao nibs add a very subtle but welcome bitter note that works very well with rose.

The quantities here are modest. To be honest, I developed this with expensive organic petals that I bought online, as I don't have enough roses in my garden. But if you are in possession of more than a fairy's bed worth of petals (lucky you!) then simply scale the recipe up and make more. Just make sure, if you are using home-grown petals, that they have not been sprayed or grown near a busy road.

MAKES 200ML / 6¾FL OZ
60g / 2¼oz rose petals
160g / 5¾oz caster [superfine] sugar
2 Tbsp lemon juice
180ml / 6fl oz water, plus 1 Tbsp
1 Tbsp cacao nibs

Place the petals in a bowl, sprinkle over 40g / 1½oz of the sugar, half the lemon juice and the 1 tablespoon of water. Massage the sugar into the petals until they are crushed and releasing wafts of ambrosial scent. Cover with plastic wrap and chill for 2 hours.

Place the remaining sugar in a small pan with the remaining 180ml / 6fl oz water and the remaining lemon juice and stir over a medium heat for 2 minutes, or until the sugar has dissolved. Add the rose petals, poke them under the sugar syrup and gently simmer, stirring occasionally, for 30 minutes, or until the mixture is reduced and thickened.

Stir in the cacao nibs then transfer to a clean jar and seal with the lid. This jam will last for a couple of weeks in the fridge.

Note: To sterilize the jar, place a clean jar and lid on a baking sheet in an oven preheated to 120°C / 250°F / Gas mark ½ for at least 20 minutes. Add the jam to the hot jar while it's still warm.

I adore good chocolate spread: it evokes memories of summer holidays with my family in Italy and France, when breakfast is gloriously leisurely and indulgent, so it seems strange that chocolate hazelnut spread was actually born out of scarcity. In the early 1800s, the Italian city of Turin was one of the chocolate capitals of Europe, famed for its chocolate houses and skilled chocolatiers. But during the naval blockades imposed by Napoleon during the Napoleonic wars, supplies of chocolate into Piedmont, the region of which Turin is capital, were severely restricted. The story goes that a chocolate maker called Michele Prochet came up with the idea to bulk out the little chocolate he had with local hazelnuts.

This eventually prompted chocolate maker Pietro Ferrero (founder of the Ferrero company) to create a solid block of hazelnut chocolate called *gianduja*: in the 1940s, Italian mothers would cut a slice off and place it between slices of bread as a snack for their children. The company later developed a soft, spreadable version called *Giandujot Supercrema*, which was revamped in the 1960s and renamed to the infinitely more pronounceable *Nutella*.

My version of chocolate spread is made with tahini, a gloriously unctuous paste made from ground sesame seeds, and I love the savoury edge it imparts to chocolate. A note about tahini: this recipe works best with a new jar, because the stuff at the bottom of an opened, half-used one tends to be too thick to work well. Ideally, give a new jar a really good stir so the oil is mixed in and the tahini is lovely and runny. This recipe can—indeed should—be made to your own personal chocolate spread preferences, so add a little more tahini, sugar or cocoa to taste.

MAKES ABOUT 200ML / 6¾FL OZ
200g/7oz tahini
80g/2¾oz icing [confectioners']
  sugar, sifted

50g/1¾oz cocoa powder, sifted
good pinch of sea salt flakes
1–4 Tbsp sesame oil (not toasted),
  as needed

This is less a recipe and more of an assembly job. Place the tahini, icing sugar and cocoa powder in a medium mixing bowl. Stir by hand or use electric beaters until everything is combined. Slowly beat in enough of the sesame oil to create the consistency of chocolate spread you prefer.

The spread will keep well in a sealed jar for 2 weeks in the fridge.

SPICY BARBECUE SAUCE

Rich, tasty and with a delicious spicy kick, this sauce is perfect served with all kinds of barbecued meats, particularly steak, burgers and sausages. The chocolate notes really enhance the charred, caramelized flavours created on the barbecue.

MAKES ABOUT 500ML / 17FL OZ

400ml / 13½fl oz passata [strained tomatoes]
1 small red onion, chopped
2 garlic cloves, chopped
2 Tbsp tomato purée [paste]
2 tsp Dijon mustard
3 Tbsp apple cider vinegar
1 Tbsp vegetable oil
1 Tbsp harissa paste
½ tsp chipotle flakes
1 tsp sea salt flakes
½ tsp liquid smoke (optional)
1 Tbsp Worcestershire sauce or soy sauce
3 Tbsp dark brown sugar
2 Tbsp cocoa powder
250ml / 8½fl oz dilute vegetable or chicken stock
20g / ¾oz dark chocolate (70% cocoa solids), chopped

Blend all the ingredients together, except the chicken stock and chocolate, in a blender until smooth.

Transfer the mixture to a pan, add a splash of the stock and simmer, uncovered, over a medium-low heat for 30 minutes. Stir regularly, adding a splash of stock now and then, to maintain a sauce-like consistency as the mixture reduces.

Add the chocolate and bubble away for a further 5 minutes until the sauce is dark and thick. Have a taste and add more salt or chocolate to your liking. Store the sauce in a large or 2 small sterilized jar/s (page 237) and use within 2 weeks.

Chocolate Turtles—the classic US candy—came to life in the 1920s when DeMet's Candy Company in Chicago realized that pecans stuck together with caramel and covered in chocolate resembled, well... reptiles with shells. This insight proved hugely popular and they are still going strong almost a century later.

My Turtle-inspired pecan bites contain dried barberries for a juicy tang instead of caramel. I discovered that these tiny sweet and sour berries, widely used in Iranian cooking, taste wonderful paired with chocolate. They're a very versatile berry that can be used in all sorts of sweet and savoury dishes, so they're worth tracking down. However, if you can't find them, use chopped dried cranberries or sour cherries instead.

MAKES 15
1 heaped Tbsp unsalted butter
¼ tsp ground cinnamon
120g/4¼oz pecans
100g/3½oz dark chocolate (between
  55–60% cocoa solids), chopped
20g/¾oz dried barberries
sea salt flakes, for sprinkling

Preheat the oven to 150°C/300°F/Gas mark 2 and line a rimmed baking sheet with baking paper.

Melt the butter in a small pan, then stir in the cinnamon. Tip the pecans onto the baking sheet, pour over the melted butter and toss to coat. Roast for 8–10 minutes, stirring the nuts halfway through, until lightly toasted. Remove from the oven and, when cool enough to handle, roughly chop, but not too much, as you want to retain lots of large bits.

Meanwhile, melt the chocolate in a heatproof bowl set over a pan of barely simmering water, making sure the bottom of the bowl does not touch the water. Remove the bowl from the pan, add the pecans and barberries and stir until the nuts and fruit are coated. (Alternatively, use the hairdryer method on page 43 to melt the chocolate and keep it in temper.)

Line a baking sheet with baking paper, scoop up heaped tablespoons of the mixture and drop them onto the prepared baking sheet in neat mounds. Leave to cool for 10 minutes, then sprinkle with sea salt flakes. Leave to cool completely and harden, about 30 minutes.

SWEET DUKKAH

I'm a huge fan of dukkah, the Egyptian condiment made from nuts, seeds, herbs and spices. It's typically used as a dip for bread anointed with olive oil, but I shower it on eggs, salad and soft cheese, for example, to ramp up the flavour and add crunch. This sweet version is equally delicious and versatile: sprinkle it over yogurt, porridge [oatmeal], stewed fruit or — my favourite — hot buttered toast.

MAKES ABOUT 200G / 7OZ

60g/2¼oz pistachios
60g/2¼oz skinless blanched almonds
2 Tbsp honey
75g/2¾oz mixed seeds, including
  sesame seeds
1½ tsp fennel seeds
¼ tsp ground cumin seeds

¼ tsp ground coriander
1 tsp ground cinnamon
1 tsp caster [superfine] sugar
3 Tbsp cacao nibs, roughly crushed
  in a spice grinder
pinch of coarse sea salt
4 Tbsp dried rose petals

Preheat the oven to 180°C/350°F/Gas mark 4 and line a rimmed baking sheet with baking paper. Let the paper overhang the sides so you can lift it out when the nuts are cooked.

Add the pistachios and almonds to the prepared sheet, drizzle with the honey and stir to coat. Spread out in a single layer and roast for 10 minutes, or until golden, stirring the nuts halfway through to ensure even cooking. Keep an eye on the nuts towards the end of the roasting time, as they will burn easily at this point.

Remove from the oven, lift out the nuts on the paper and set aside on a wire rack to cool completely. Once completely cool, pulse in a food processor to make a rough rubble of finely ground and larger pieces of nuts.

Meanwhile, toast the mixed seeds and fennel seeds in a dry frying pan until they start to smell toasty. Tip into a mixing bowl, then add all the remaining ingredients, including the blitzed nuts but not the rose petals. Mix well so all the ingredients are evenly distributed, then fold in the rose petals. Store in an airtight jar for up to a month.

"Not a single company or government is anywhere near reaching the sector-wide objective of the elimination of child labour, and not even near their commitments of a 70% reduction of child labour by 2020." — Cocoa Barometer 2018

I'm ashamed to admit that until I started researching this book, I gave scant thought to chocolate's journey from bean to bar. If I considered it at all, my mind conjured Wonka-esque images of vats of molten chocolate, conveyor belts of bonbons and factories imbued with the scent of cocoa. I now understand the unpalatable truth: behind most chocolate bars are humans, the very young through to the very old, who toil for scandalously little reward, never knowing the pleasure of chocolate themselves. And extreme poverty sits at the root of a raft of problems associated with the cocoa industry. Child labour, deforestation, human rights violations and the destruction of wildlife are also among the hidden costs of every cheap chocolate bar. An exaggeration? Sadly not.

Just as it was with sugar, coffee and tobacco, exploitation and egregious labour practices have been features of the global chocolate trade since the beginning. In the early seventeenth century, the indigenous people of the Americas and the West Indies were coerced by colonial settlers — often missionaries — to pick cacao for export to Europe. When the 'natives' proved uncooperative or were wiped out by European diseases, they were simply replaced by slaves; ships from colonies in Africa made the notorious Middle Passage crossing and 'poured their wretched human cargo' into the cacao plantations to toil.

Portugal, Spain, France, Britain, Holland, Denmark and others took part in this lucrative three-way trading system: ships carried manufactured goods to Africa to be bartered for slaves, who were then shipped in unspeakably appalling conditions to sugar, cacao and tobacco plantations in New World colonies. It is estimated that 12.5 million enslaved Africans were transported to the Americas between 1500 and 1866. And thus, wealthy Europeans had plenty of chocolate (sweetened with slave-grown sugar) to sip in their clubs, drawing rooms and boudoirs.

The Portuguese were the first to have the commercial foresight, grotesque as it was, to turn the tables and transport cacao to the slaves. A few years before Brazil's independence in 1823, the Portuguese monarchy ordered cacao seedlings to be shipped from there to São Tomé and Principe, its tiny island holdings off the coast of West Africa, along with the forced labour production system. The plants thrived and cacao soon spread to the colonies of Ghana and Nigeria (British), Cote d'Ivoire (French) and Cameroon (German). The British also carried cacao to Ceylon (Sri Lanka), the Dutch to the East Indies (Java and Sumatra) and Spain to the Philippines. Cacao circumnavigated the globe on the back of slave labour.

Slave trading was officially outlawed over the course of the nineteenth century (although the ban was often flouted). But slavery continued, virtually under the radar, in the cacao plantations of West Africa, until scandal rocked the chocolate industry.

Cadbury's, the British chocolate giant run by a Quaker family who championed the abolition of slavery and touted justice and welfare for all, found itself at the centre of controversy. Reports emerged that forced labour was still being practised in São Tomé, where Cadbury's sourced much of its cacao. Deborah Cadbury writes in her book *Chocolate Wars* that the firm was aware of labour abuses for years before the allegations became public but had actively been trying to bring about change through diplomatic and political channels, while continuing to buy cacao grown on the island.

In 1908, London's *Evening Standard* newspaper accused Cadbury's of hypocrisy and the firm sued for libel. Cadbury's argued it had tried to use its leverage as a buyer to change the system, something it could not do if it boycotted São Tomé cacao. The jury upheld Cadbury's libel claim but awarded 'contemptuous damages' of one farthing (around 30p/40 cents in today's money). The jury was clearly unimpressed by Cadbury's approach; despite its opposition to slavery, the company had still profited from it.

Slavery might be outlawed but exploitation has endured. In 2001, a landmark film by Brian Woods and Kate Blewett called *Slavery: A Global Investigation,* inspired by Kevin Bales' book *Disposable People,* shifted the issue into the public spotlight again.

They discovered child labourers who were being appallingly treated on cacao plantations in Côte d'Ivoire. And in 2018, the situation is still grim for the millions of people who barely scratch a living working in West Africa's cacao industry. The region now supplies around three-quarters of the world's cacao, most from plantations in Côte d'Ivoire and Ghana. Here, farmers with smallholdings of less than 5 hectares produce the cacao that goes into the cheap confectionery bars of large chocolate brands such as Mars, Mondelēz, Nestlé and Hershey. Few have ever seen or tasted chocolate.

According to Cocoa Barometer 2018, a report assembled by NGOs involved in sustainable cacao production, more than half of cacao farmers in Côte d'Ivoire earn the equivalent of $US0.78 per day or less, below the World Bank's extreme poverty line. Only 7 per cent earn a decent standard of living. There are now real concerns that the younger generation is abandoning cacao farming for jobs that afford them a decent life in the cities. Who will be left to grow cacao? What's more, the cacao farmers left behind are old, and lack the necessary financial resources and drive to innovate.

In October 2018, I attended an Academy of Chocolate conference in London, entitled A World Without Chocolate, where world experts explored the crisis facing the global cacao trade. The overall message was depressing. Expert after expert warned that the concentration of cacao production in West Africa posed a real threat to chocolate supplies. Climate change, deforestation, pests, disease and poverty needed to be overcome to keep the world's appetite for chocolate sated. But will this be possible when farmers are living in poverty, using production methods that haven't changed for 50 years and operating in an industry tightly controlled by government?

The causes of structural poverty among cacao farmers in West Africa are complex. Just a few decades ago, cacao farming was an elite profession, but no longer. As global production has grown to keep pace with demand for cheap chocolate, farmers' incomes have plummeted. Desperately poor, they have little bargaining power to improve their lot in a market controlled by a handful of powerful multinational companies. And the cocoa supply chain lacks transparency, with some suppliers and traders operating behind the scenes, unaccountable for their actions.

Cocoa prices are also highly volatile, and many farmers have no protection against the fluctuations. For example, between

September 2016 and February 2017, West African smallholders already struggling with poverty saw their cacao incomes fall by as much as 40 per cent. Overproduction and stagnant demand for chocolate globally had created a perfect storm for prices to plunge. At the time of writing, cocoa prices had climbed again, but farmers remain vulnerable.

Poverty drives child labour. More than 2 million children, some of them very young and some believed to have been trafficked, still toil in the cacao fields of Côte d'Ivoire and Ghana, often engaged in dangerous work. In 2001, the US congress came close to passing a new law requiring all cocoa products to carry 'slave-free' labels. But after intense lobbying, the chocolate industry managed to block the legislation, agreeing instead to the non-binding Harkin-Engel Protocol. This was designed to end the worst forms of forced child labour in cacao production by 2005, but that deadline has been repeatedly pushed back, and now stands at 2020.

The collapse in the price of cacao is linked to increased supply: global production has risen four-fold since 1960, with native forests destroyed to make way for ever more cacao plantations. In West Africa, more than 90 per cent of the original forests are gone and wildlife populations — notably chimpanzees and elephants — have been decimated. "This can be equally attributed to corporate disinterest in the environmental effects of the supply of cheap cacao, and to an almost completely absent government enforcement of environmentally protected areas," Cocoa Barometer 2018 reports. Large-scale deforestation driven by the chocolate industry has also been discovered in Indonesia, Cameroon, Peru and Ecuador.

Increased production has also seen a decline in cacao diversity. In simple terms, this means the most complex, full-flavoured genetic strains of beans are making way for blander varieties that are more productive and easier to grow. As well, cacao production is threatened by climate change. Scientists predict that a rise in temperature and no accompanying increase in rainfall will reduce the humidity in cacao-producing countries like Côte d'Ivoire, Ghana, and Indonesia. As a result, viable land for cacao production will shrink significantly by 2050.

So what's being done to resolve the problems and what can chocolate lovers do to play their part? Big chocolate companies are now publicly committed to tackling child labour and the other challenges linked to cacao production. There is an emerging consensus that the gap between poverty-level cacao farming and wealthy chocolate consumers must be bridged. Mondelēz International, for example, which owns the Cadbury brand, launched its Cocoa Life programme in 2012, a $US400 million strategy to protect the land, tackle child labour and improve farmer livelihoods. And Barry Callebaut, one of the world's largest cacao producers and grinders, launched its Forever Chocolate initiative in 2016, which aims to make sustainable chocolate the norm by 2025, including the eradication of child labour.

But chocolate companies can't do it on their own, a truth recognized by the International Cocoa Initiative (ICI), a non-profit foundation that brings together industry and local communities in Ghana and Côte d'Ivoire. The ICI focuses on improving education opportunities and empowering women, as gender inequality in West Africa is strongly linked with children going out to work. Progress is being made — but painfully slowly.

Public awareness of the ethical issues endemic to cheap chocolate production is also growing. Big manufacturers including Nestlé, Hershey and Mars, have faced a number of class action lawsuits in the US (unsuccessful or ongoing at the time of writing), over their failure to inform consumers that cocoa in their products may have come from child or slave labour.

But what else can consumers do? There isn't an easy answer. Buying Fairtrade chocolate does not guarantee that farmers receive a living income or that child labour has not been used, although the premium you pay for bars that carry this certification is invested in local businesses and communities.

There is no guarantee that cacao grown outside West Africa is ethically produced, but experts generally agree that it probably does not involve forced or child labour. However, the livelihoods of millions of farmers and their families in West Africa depend on the cacao industry, so boycotting cheap chocolate is not a solution, either. Should we be prepared to pay more for chocolate if this guarantees a decent living for cacao farmers?

The growth of the fine chocolate market has raised the volume on the global conversation about price, flavour and ethics in the industry. Many of these craft chocolate makers explain the origin of their cacao beans on the wrapper, raising public awareness about cacao varieties and giving growers the recognition that they deserve. Moreover, fine chocolate makers often buy their cacao directly from farmers and cooperatives, and pay a premium for high-quality, ethically sourced beans.

Some experts working to improve the sustainability of the cocoa sector say consumers should consider eating more dark chocolate, as opting for bars with a higher cocoa content might result in farmers selling more of what they grow and potentially boost their incomes. Others urge chocolate lovers to ask questions about the origin of the bars they buy and whether they were ethically produced.

At the Academy of Chocolate conference I asked several experts what consumers could do to help and they were unanimous: choose chocolate for flavour, quality and provenance not the cheapest price tag. "We have to persuade people to pay more for their chocolate bars," one expert said. "It's as simple as that."

INDEX

BIBLIOGRAPHY

Peter Barham, *The Science of Cooking*, Springer-Verlag (2001)

Stephen T Beckett, *The Science of Chocolate*, RSC Publishing (2009)

Deborah Cadbury, *Chocolate Wars*, HarperPress (2011)

Sophie and Michael Coe, *The True History of Chocolate,* Thames & Hudson (2013)

Sarah Jane Evans, *Chocolate Unwrapped*, Pavilion Books (2010)

Louis Evan Grivetti and Howard-Yana Shapiro (editors), *Chocolate: History, Culture and Heritage*, John Wiley & Sons (2009)

Sara Jayne-Stanes, *Chocolate: The Definitive Guide*, Grub Street (2005)

Diana Kennedy, *The Essential Cuisines of Mexico*, Clarkson Potter (2000)

David Lebovitz, *The Great Book of Chocolate*, Ten Speed Press (2004)

Kristy Leissle, *Cocoa*, Polity Press (2018)

Nick Malgieri, *Chocolate: From Simple Cookies to Extravagant Showstoppers*, HarperCollins (1998)

T. Masonis, G D'Alesandre, L. Vega and M. Gore, *Making Chocolate: From Bean to Bar to S'more*, Clarkson Potter (2017)

Harold McGee, *On Food and Cooking: The Science and Lore of the Kitchen*, Scribner (2004)

Marcia and Frederic Morton, *Chocolate: An Illustrated History*, Crown Publishers (1986)

Sarah Moss and Alexander Badenoch, *Chocolate: A Global History,* Reaktion Books (2009)

Maricel E. Presilla, *The New Taste of Chocolate*, Ten Speed Press (2001)

Emma Robertson, *Chocolate, Women and Empire,* Manchester University Press (2009)

Niki Segnit, *The Flavour Thesaurus*, Bloomsbury Publishing (2010)

Simran Sethi, *Bread, Wine, Chocolate: The Slow Loss of Foods We Love*, HarperCollins (2015)

Paul A. Young, *Adventures with Chocolate*, Kyle Books (2009)

ACKNOWLEDGEMENTS

There are so many people to thank for their support, knowledge and wisdom.

Thanks to Sarah Lavelle for allowing my idea to blossom and to Céline Hughes, the most calm and lovely of editors, for letting me write the book I wanted to write, and ensuring it was the very best it could be. Also thanks to Kathy Steer for her patience and skill in making sense of my words. To Yuki Sugiura, Aya Nishimura, Alexander Breeze and Claire Rochford—love and salutes for your superhuman efforts in creating stunning chocolate photographs during a record-breaking heatwave. We will laugh about it one day. I'm also indebted to the extraordinary folk at A Practice for Everyday Life for the book's stunning design.

I am indebted to Martin Christy, co-founder of the International Institute of Chocolate and Cacao Tasting, chocolate tasting tutor Cat Black, and scientist and chocolate expert Dr Alex Rast for sharing their vast knowledge of chocolate. Also thanks to Spencer Hyman, founder of online chocolate purveyor Cocoa Runners, for his delicious and valuable insights.

Thanks to the Guittard chocolate company, which provided chocolate for recipe testing. The wonderful Chris and Joanna Brennan from Pump Street Chocolate also provided their wonderful chocolate for our photo shoot, and shared much cocoa knowledge: thank you. Also many thanks to Paul A. Young for chatting to me about chocolate and flavour. And thanks to Kerry Witt, founder of Chocolate by Miss Witt, for teaching me about tempering.

For help with chocolate in Italian cooking past and present, thanks so much to Rosemarie Scavo, Lucia Hannau (@turinepi), Katia Amore (@lovesicily), Emiko Davies (@emikodavies) and Francine Segan—your knowledge was invaluable. Similarly, thank you Rachel McCormack for your insights into chocolate in Catalan cookery.

Hugs to Nicola Miller and Kate Young for sharing your stupendous knowledge of chocolate and books, and to Peter Barham for his science insights.

Huge thanks to my agent Heather Holden-Brown for your support, hard work and persistence. Also to Diana Henry—I am grateful, as ever, for your encouragement: it means a great deal.

Love and deepest thanks go to chef Martha Ortiz, whose love for and knowledge about chocolate in Mexican cookery were inspiring. You helped me realize that chocolate is more than food (although, when it comes to eating it, there is no mole like yours).

Finally, thanks to my in-house support team and loyal outriders, Adam, Ruby and Ben. Your faith in me is what made this book possible.

Publishing Director: Sarah Lavelle
Commissioning Editor: Céline Hughes
Design and Illustration: A Practice for Everyday Life
Design Manager: Claire Rochford
Photographer: Yuki Sugiura
Food Stylist: Aya Nishimura
Prop Stylist: Alexander Breeze
Production Director: Vincent Smith
Production Controller: Nikolaus Ginelli

Published in 2019 by Quadrille,
an imprint of Hardie Grant Publishing

Quadrille
52–54 Southwark Street
London SE1 1UN
quadrille.com

Cataloguing in Publication Data: a catalogue record for this book is available from the British Library.

ISBN 978 1 78713 260 3

Printed in China

Text credits: page 6 excerpt(s) from CHOCOLAT: A NOVEL by Joanne Harris (USA), copyright © 1999 by Joanne Harris. Used by permission of Viking Books, an imprint of Penguin Publishing Group, a division of Penguin Random House LLC. All rights reserved; 33 The Loveliest Chocolate Shop in Paris © Jenny Colgan; 192 excerpt(s) from CHARLIE AND THE CHOCOLATE FACTORY by Roald Dahl (USA), text copyright © 1964, renewed 1992 by Roald Dahl Nominee Limited. Used by permission of Alfred A. Knopf, an imprint of Random House Children's Books, a division of Penguin Random House LLC. All rights reserved; 192 (UK) © The Roald Dahl Story Company Limited. The publisher has made every effort to trace the copyright holders. We apologise in advance for any unintentional omissions and would be pleased to insert the appropriate acknowledgement in any subsequent edition.

Picture credits: page 8 Mary Evans Picture Library; 14 Lordprice Collection/ Alamy Stock Photo; 21 Mary Evans Picture Library; 24 Mary Evans / Retrograph Collection; 30 Courtesy of The Advertising Archives; 34 Mary Evans / INTERFOTO / TV-Yesterday~~; 41 Mary Evans / Retrograph Collection; 46 Mary Evans Picture Library